Keto Wood Pellet Smoker and Grill Cookbook for Beginners

600-Day Tasty, Low-Carb Ketogenic Diet Recipes for Perfect Smoking

Waron Hezen

© Copyright 2021 Waron Hezen- All Rights Reserved.

In no way is it legal to reproduce, duplicate, or transmit any part of this document by either electronic means or in printed format. Recording of this publication is strictly prohibited, and any storage of this material is not allowed unless with written permission from the publisher. All rights reserved.

The information provided herein is stated to be truthful and consistent, in that any liability, regarding inattention or otherwise, by any usage or abuse of any policies, processes, or directions contained within is the solitary and complete responsibility of the recipient reader. Under no circumstances will any legal liability or blame be held against the publisher for any reparation, damages, or monetary loss due to the information herein, either directly or indirectly.

Respective authors own all copyrights not held by the publisher.

Legal Notice:

This book is copyright protected. This is only for personal use. You cannot amend, distribute, sell, use, quote or paraphrase any part of the content within this book without the consent of the author or copyright owner. Legal action will be pursued if this is breached.

Disclaimer Notice:

Please note the information contained within this document is for educational and entertainment purposes only. Every attempt has been made to provide accurate, up-to-date and reliable, complete information. No warranties of any kind are expressed or implied. Readers acknowledge that the author is not engaging in the rendering of legal, financial, medical or professional advice.

By reading this document, the reader agrees that under no circumstances are we responsible for any losses, direct or indirect, which are incurred as a result of the use of information contained within this document, including, but not limited to, errors, omissions, or inaccuracies.

Table of contents

Introduction 5
Chapter 1: Keto Diet Basics 6
    What is Keto Diet? 6
    How does Keto Diet Work? 6
    How to Know Whether Your Body is in Ketosis or Not? 6
    The Advantages of Keto Diet 8
    Tips and Tricks for Successful Keto Journey 9
Chapter 2: Wood Pellet Smoker and Grill Basics 11
    How to Use the Grill 11
    Getting Started with Your Grills 11
    Shutdown Procedure 12
    Temperature Settings 12
    Cleaning the Grills 13
Chapter 3: Poultry Recipes 14
    Fruit Stuffed Goose 14   Glazed Chicken Drumsticks 22
    Crispy Duck 16   Coffee Flavored Chicken 23
    Sweet & Spicy Chicken Thighs 17   Glazed Turkey Breast 24
    Buttered Turkey 18   Glazed Chicken Wings 26
    Rosemary Cornish Hens 19   Chicken Casserole 27
    Bacon Wrapped Chicken Breasts 20
Chapter 4: Beef Recipes 29
    Mustard Beef Short Ribs 29   Beef Tenderloin 39
    Brandy Beef Tenderloin 31   Beef Stuffed Bell Peppers 40
    BBQ Meatloaf 33   Spicy Chuck Roast 42
    Sweet & Spicy Beef Brisket 35   BBQ Spiced Flank Steak 43
    Herbed Prime Rib Roast 37   Beef Rump Roast 44
Chapter 5: Pork Recipes 45
    Glazed Pork Rack of Ribs 45   Simple Pork Belly 53
    Sweet & Spicy Pork Ribs 47   BBQ Rub Pork Chops 54
    Sweet & Spicy Pork Chops 49   Jam Glazed Sausage 56
    Spiced Pork Butt Roast 50   Glazed Pork Tenderloin 57
    Sweet & Spiced Glazed Ham 51   Honey Glazed ham 58

Chapter 6: Lamb Recipes 60

Herbed Rack of Lamb 60
Stuffed Leg of Lamb 62
Simple Lamb Chops 64
Cheesy Lamb Burgers 65
Cola Flavored Rack of Lamb................. 66
Wine Flavored Leg of Lamb................. 67
Buttermilk Brined Shoulder Chops..... 68
Seasoned Lamb Shoulder..................... 70
Sweet & Tangy Braised Lamb Shank.. 71
Lemony & Spicy Lamb Shoulder......... 72

Chapter 7: Fish & Seafood Recipes 74

Rosemary Trout 74
Prosciutto Wrapped Scallops 76
Lemony Lobster Tails 77
Simple Mahi-Mahi 78
Wine Brined Salmon 79
Sesame Seeds Flounder 81
Citrus Salmon....................................... 82
Parsley Prawn Skewers......................... 83
Buttered Clams..................................... 84
Buttered Shrimp................................... 85

Chapter 8: Vegetarian Recipes 86

Spiced Mushrooms 86
Mac n' Cheese 87
Parmesan Cauliflower........................... 89
Mixed Veggies Combo 91
Cheesy Potato Fries 92
Baked Beans 93
Vegetarian Pot Pie 94
Tofu Skewers 96
Potato Casserole 98
Cheesy Corn 100

Chapter 9: Extra Recipes... 101

Apple Pie... 101
Rhubarb Crunch 103
Irish Soda Bread 105

Conclusion 107

Introduction

The ketogenic barbecue diet, a low-carb, high-fat way of eating, is remarkably effective at transforming people's lives, helping them shed pounds and find relief from common health conditions. The reason so many diets fail is that dieters tend to deny themselves of the things they like to eat. That leads to boredom and boredom leads to giving up because it simply becomes too hard to succeed. So if you want to lose weight you should choose a diet that allows you to eat at least some of the things you enjoy, and this is where the ketogenic barbecue diet stands out above the rest.

In this book, Keto Wood Pellet Smoker and Grill Cookbook for Beginners, anyone who enjoys eating meat will discover that succeeding with their weight loss program will be much easier. Complete with an introduction to the ketogenic barbecue diet and where meat fits in with this, as well as in-depth recipe ideas that include nutritional values and full instructions, this book includes all the basic recipes you'll need to make your favorite dishes, and we've included a lot of tips and tricks to get you started.

So if you are wondering if the Keto barbecue diet is for you, this is the book that will help you overcome all your concerns and set you on the path to a healthier and stronger you!

Chapter 1: Keto Diet Basics

What is Keto Diet?

The Keto diet is one of the most effective and popular diet plans comes with long term health benefits. Keto is a low-carb, high-fat diet plan that allows a moderate amount of protein during the diet period. Keto is not just a diet plan it completely changes your daily food eating habit towards natural and healthy food consumption. Generally, our body depends on glucose (carb) for energy to perform day-to-day activities. When the glucose level in our body increases the excess glucose is converted into glycogens and stored in liver and body cells.

The Keto diet is a low carb diet, so the carb consumption is reduced during a keto diet. Due to this glucose level is decreased and our body finds out the alternative source for energy. It breaks down fats for energy. This state of the body is also called ketosis. It is one of the metabolic processes where fats are broken down and produce ketones for energy. These ketones provide an endless source of energy to our body. The Keto diet is one of the most followed diets for weight loss purposes. It not only maintains your healthy body weight but also improves your physical and mental health.

How does Keto Diet Work?

In general, our body uses glucose (carb) as a primary source of energy. When we reduce the intake of carbohydrates during the diet, glucose level automatically reduces. In this condition, our body shifts itself to break down fats for energy in the absence of carbohydrates (glucose). In fat breaking process some fatty acids are released our livers convert these fatty acids into ketones.

Ketones are produced due to a chemical process when our body burns fat for energy instead of glucose. Most of the body organs and tissues use these ketones as an alternative source of energy. Ketones are one of the best fuels for our brain they fulfill more than 70% of our brain energy needs. The lack of glucose pushes our body into the state of ketosis.

How to Know Whether Your Body is in Ketosis or Not?

There are several sign and symptoms and methods which indicate that your body is in the state of ketosis or not. These signs, symptoms, and methods are mention as follows.

- **Increase in thirst and dry mouth**

This is one of the common side effects noticed when you are following a keto diet. In this state, your body loses excess sodium and water, so it is recommended that add 2 to 4 grams of sodium into your diet to balancing the electrolyte level into your body. This will also increase the urination process and increase thirst. These signs and symptoms indicate that your body is in a state of ketosis.

- **Keto Breath or Bad Breath**

This is one of the common side effects noticed during the first week of the keto diet. When your body breaks down fats for energy, in this process acetone are release and produce a fruity smell or nail polish remover like smell having the bad breath symptoms. This is happening due to keto diet plan adaptation. Keto breath or bad breath symptoms will indicate that your body is in the state of ketosis.

- **Rapid Weight Loss**

This happens when your body breaks down fats for energy instead of glucose (carb). If you notice that your weight is rapidly reduced during the first week of the keto diet, then. Rapid weight loss is another sign and symptom that indicates that your body is in the state of ketosis.

- **Blood Test**

A blood test is one of the common and accurate methods used to measure the ketones level. It is one of the few expensive methods of measuring blood ketones levels in diabetic patients. The blood test method is similar to a glucometer test. In this case, you need to use a keto meter instead of a glucometer with a lancet pen and test strips. If the keto meter shows reading 0.5 and 3 mml/L which indicates that your body is in the state of ketosis.

- **Ketostix**

Ketostix is one of the accurate and inexpensive ways to check your ketones level in the urine. You just need to collect the urine in a clean urine container then dip the Ketostix and shake to remove the excess urine from the stick and wait for 15 seconds. After 15 minutes you have noticed that Ketostix color is changed. To measure the ketones level just follow the color guide match with your strip color to check the ketosis.

- **Increase focus and energy**

Most people notice that tiredness and sickness during the first few days of the keto diet. When your body uses ketones for energy. It not only improves your physical health but also improves your focus and energy. This is happening because 70% of brain energy needs are fulfilled by ketones. This is another sign which indicates that your body is in the state of ketosis.

The Advantages of Keto Diet

The keto diet is one of the most popular diets for years comes with various kinds of health benefits some of them are described as follows.

- **Rapid Weight loss**

If you are overweight and want to reduce the extra weight rapidly then the keto diet is one of the best choices to maintain your healthy body weight. During the keto diet, our body breaks down fats for energy instead of glucose. Due to this fat breaking process, you have notice rapid weight loss. The diet allows a moderate number of proteins, so you don't feel hungrier during the diet period. This will help to reduce your bodyweight rapidly and gives you long term weight loss benefits.

- **Improve your Brain Functions**

Keto diet is low carb diet, due to low carb consumption glucose level decreases and our body finds out alternative energy source by breaking the fats for energy. During the fat breaking process some chemical releases. Our liver converts these chemicals into ketones. To perform day-to-day operations our body use ketones as an energy source. It fulfills more than 70% of brain energy needs. Most of the study and research proves that ketones improve focus, attention and memory functions.

- **Effective on various medical conditions**

The keto diet is not only used for weight loss purposes but also used to treat various medical conditions like Alzheimer's, Parkinson's, type-2 diabetes, heart-related disease, blood pressure, and also in epilepsy conditions.

- **Improves Cholesterol Levels**

The keto diet is a low-carb high-fat diet. It allows you to consume healthy fats during the diet period. Healthy fats are responsible to improve the HDL (good cholesterol) level. Carbohydrates are one of the main reasons to increase the LDL (bad cholesterol) level. The Keto diet is a low-carb diet, so it decreases the LDL level and also reduces the risk of heart-related disease.

- **Control Appetite**

The keto diet is a low carb, high fat, and moderate protein diet. The diet is enriching with all essential nutrients the moderate protein in diet which helps prevent an increase in appetite. You never feel hungry after eating healthy keto diet food.

- **Longevity**

Keto diet is responsible to increase your lifespan. The keto diet allows you to consume healthy notorious and antioxidant-rich foods. This will help to cures various health-related problems that occur due to the consumption of unhealthy and poor diet. The scientific studies prove that the peoples who follow the keto diet can result in a significant drop in oxidative stress level. It also reduces the risk of diabetes, heart disease, and obesity and improves lifespan.

- **Increase in energy levels**

The keto diet shifts your body to breakdown fats for energy instead of glucose. During the fat breaking, process chemicals are released, and our liver converts it into ketones. Ketones provide energy to our body organ and tissues and long-lasting energy source to our body. Due to an increase in energy level, you feel active and fully energized the whole day.

Tips and Tricks for Successful Keto Journey

The following tips and tricks are helpful to complete your keto journey.

1. **Limit Daily Carb Consumption**

To stay in ketosis, it is recommended to consume 10 to 30 grams of carb daily. If you are an active person and doing hard exercise for 5 to 6 days a week then you can increase carb consumption. Don't eat too much carb it may build up glycogen storage.

2. **Eat healthy fats**

During the keto diet, it is recommended to eat healthy fats like avocado oil, olive oil, coconut oil, etc. avoid unhealthy fats like vegetable oil, sunflower oil, canola oil, etc. Healthy fat consumption will help to boost ketone levels in your body and keep your body in a ketosis state.

3. **Get enough sleep**

Due to Inadequate sleep, you feel hunger and it is one of the bad signs for your weight loss process. To stay in ketosis during the keto diet you need not only enough sleep but also get better quality sleep. Better quality means you should sleep in a cool and darkroom. The room temperature is maintained at 65 F and you need to sleep at least 7 hours a daily night to get complete enough sleep.

4. **Consume Moderate Protein**

In the keto diet our body breaks down fats for energy. In this fat breaking process some healthy muscles and fats. An adequate amount of protein consumption will help to repair this muscle and also maintain muscle mass. As per your body weight, it is recommended to consume 0.75 grams of protein per pound.

5. **Regular exercise**

Regular exercise during the keto diet will keep you energized throughout the day. It also increases the ketones level and decreases the carb from your body. Regular exercise keeps you fit and also maintains your blood sugar level.

6. **Use MCT oils**

Use coconut oil which contains healthy fats called MCT (Medium Chain Triglycerides). It is easily absorbed by the liver and converts into ketones. MCT oils provide an instant source of energy to our body and are converted into ketones. MCTs travel fast into your body and enter into your body cells without broken.

7. **Stay Hydrated**

When you follow the keto diet, it is important to keep your body hydrated. During the diet period, your body loses glycogens through the urination process. These glycogens hold 5 parts of water, so your body is dehydrated during the diet. To keep your body hydrated you need to consume smoothies, coffee, or tea during the diet period.

Chapter 2: Wood Pellet Smoker and Grill Basics

How to Use the Grill

If you are using the Grill for the very first time, then here are some initial steps that you need to take to make your grill operational.

1. Remove heat baffle, grease tray, and grill racks, from the grill.
2. Now open lid over pellet hopper and check to see if it is clean from contamination.
3. Plug in the appliance and switch it ON while keeping the Controller dial in the shutdown cycle position.
4. Then rotate the temperature dial to the smoke position.
5. Now see if the auger is turning slowly in the grill.
6. Keep your hand above the firepot, and check if the air is flowing.
7. Check if the ignition rod is getting dull red in 4 minutes. Avoid touching this hot rod.
8. Finally, add some pellets to the hopper and rotate the dial to High setting. Wait for the pellets to reach to the firepot.
9. When the pellets start dropping into the fire pot, turn the dial to the smoke indicator then wait for the pellets to ignite.
10. Once the pellets reach to a full flame, turn the dial to the shutdown position and leave the grill for cooling.
11. These steps help you make the fire inside the grill, and they must be repeated before every session when new pellets are introduced into the grill.
12. Now your grill is ready for normal grilling session, so you can place the grease tray, heat baffle, and grill rack back in the grill.

Getting Started with Your Grills

- **Basic Steps to Grill and Smoke**

Now that the grill is set up and ready to use, you can follow these steps to cook a variety of meals in your Grill:

1. Open the lid of the grill.
2. Switch on the plugged-in grill while keeping its controller dial in the shutdown cycle.
3. Then turn the dial to smoke position, and soon, you will hear a roaring sound of smoke-producing inside. Then close the lid.

4. Rotate the dial to the required temperature settings then wait for 10 minutes or more to allow the grill to heat up.
5. Place the food inside, after greasing the grilling grates with cooking oil, if needed.
6. Do not frequently open the Grill lid, or the required temperature will not be maintained inside the grill.
7. The grill always takes some time to reach the desired temperature, so be patient and give it the due time.

Shutdown Procedure

Once the grilling or smoking session is complete, you need to carry out this whole shutdown procedure so that the grill would stop producing heat.

1. To do so, first, turn the controller dial to the shutdown position.
2. After this step, the auger will automatically stop turning and rotating.
3. But at this point, the fan of the grill will keep running for the next 5-20 minutes to get rid of the heat inside the grill.
4. When the fan stops running, it is the sign to switch off the appliance and unplug it.
5. In case, if the power button switches off due to the power outage or by some accident, then immediately turn on the grill and turn its dial to the smoke position.
6. And then turn the dial to the shutdown position after minutes of this operation.

Temperature Settings

Keep a few things in mind while adjusting the temperature of the grill. If you want to switch it to low temperatures from high temperatures, the grill will take a longer time. So it is better to turn the dial to the Shutdown cycle.

New pellets are automatically introduced to the fire pot when the temperature starts to drop below the set temperature setting, and that keeps the temperature maintained without your efforts.

But when the new pellets reach a full ignition, they can even raise the temperature above the desired temperature. So, you can reduce the heat by keeping the lid open for a while. The temperature can fluctuate a bit during the first hour of cooking, but it is quite normal.

Remember that the food receives indirect heat from the grill, so small or slight changes in the temperature will not directly affect the cooking process. The temperature of the grill is measure through the sensor fixed on the top left side of the grilling drum, so the temperature on the main grill rack remains lower than the rest of the grill.

Cleaning the Grills

The following important steps will help you clean your Grill after every cooking session. It is noteworthy here that cleaning keeps the grill in better condition. We all know that after every grilling session, a large amount of grease, soot, and ash is left behind. And if all of it is not cleaned in time, then it causes operational inefficiency for the machine.

1. Start by removing the foil from the grease tray of the Grill and wipe it off to clean its surface.
2. Remember that the longer you will leave the grease on the trays, the hard it will get to wipe it off. You can clean the trays once they are cooled enough to handle without damaging anything.
3. Clean the V-shaped drain and remove its grease too.
4. Then take the grease bucket and discard all the grease from it then wash it well with soap water.
5. To clean the grilling racks, use a pumice stone, wood scraper, or a ball of foil to gently scrape off all the food particles stuck to the grill. Avoid using the stainless-steel wire brush as it damages the ceramic coating on the grills.
6. Once the food particles are scraped off, use a wet cloth to wipe off all the grease. Wear gloves to clean the grills as they can be hot after cooking.
7. Avoid using any chemical or acidic cleaners as they also damage the ceramic coating of the grills.
8. The next step is to clean the chimney and the firepot. The ash present in the Grill drum and firepot can be cleaned using the vacuum cleaner, but you can only vacuum when the grill is cold, and it is unplugged.
9. After 4-5 sessions of grilling, remove the chimney cap an wash it with warm soapy water. Gently wipe or scrape off the soot from the chimney using BBQ wipes or other non-metallic scrubs.
10. Now using BBQ cleaning wipes or any moist cloth to wipe the grill from inside and out.
11. When the grill is not in use, keep it over and protected. The grill must not be exposed to the rain.
12. Wipe the temperature sensor gently with a BBQ cleaning wipe.
13. The food probes can be scrubbed and washed with soapy water to clean them thoroughly and keep them contamination-free.

Chapter 3: Poultry Recipes

Fruit Stuffed Goose

Preparation Time: 20 minutes
Cooking Time: 3 hours
Servings: 12

Ingredients:

- 1½ cups kosher salt
- 1 cup brown sugar
- 20 cups water
- 1 (12-pound) whole goose, giblets removed
- 1 naval orange, cut into 6 wedges
- 1 large onion, cut into 8 wedges
- 2 bay leaves
- ¼ cup juniper berries, crushed
- 12 black peppercorns
- Salt and ground black pepper, as required
- 1 apple, cut into 6 wedges
- 2-3 fresh parsley sprigs

Method:

1. Trim off any loose neck skin.
2. Then, trim the first two joints off the wings.
3. Wash the goose under cold running water and with paper towels, pat dry it.
4. With the tip of a paring knife, prick the goose all over the skin.
5. In a large pitcher, dissolve kosher salt and brown sugar in water.
6. Squeeze 3 orange wedges into brine.
7. Add goose, 4 onion wedges, bay leaves, juniper berries and peppercorns in brine and refrigerate for 24 hours.
8. Preheat the Wood Pellet Smoker and Grill on grill setting to 350 degrees F.
9. Remove the goose from brine and with paper towels, pat dry completely.
10. Season the in and outside of goose with salt and black pepper evenly.
11. Stuff the cavity with apple wedges, herbs, remaining orange and onion wedges.
12. With kitchen strings, tie the legs together loosely.
13. Place the goose onto a rack arranged in a shallow roasting pan.

14. Arrange the goose on pellet grill and cook for about 1 hour.
15. With a basting bulb, remove some of the fat from the pan and cook for about 1 hour.
16. Again, remove excess fat from the pan and cook for about ½-1 hour more.
17. Remove goose from grill and place onto a cutting board for about 20 minutes before carving.
18. With a sharp knife, cut the goose into desired-sized pieces and serve.

Nutritional Information per Serving:

- Calories 907
- Total Fat 60.3 g
- Saturated Fat 16.3 g
- Cholesterol 3865 mg
- Sodium 10000 mg
- Total Carbs 23.5 g
- Fiber 1.1 g
- Sugar 19.9 g
- Protein 63.3 g

Crispy Duck

Preparation Time: 15 minutes
Cooking Time: 4 hours 5 minutes
Servings: 6

Ingredients:

- ¾ cup honey
- ¾ cup soy sauce
- ¾ cup red wine
- 1 teaspoon paprika
- 1½ tablespoons garlic salt
- Ground black pepper, as required
- 1 (5-pound) whole duck, giblets removed and trimmed

Method:

1. Preheat the Wood Pellet Smoker and Grill on grill setting to 225-250 degrees F.
2. In a bowl, add all ingredients except for duck and mix until well combined.
3. With a fork, poke holes in the skin of the duck.
4. Coat the duck with honey mixture generously.
5. Arrange duck in pellet gill, breast side down and cook for about 4 hours, coating with honey mixture one after 2 hours.
6. Remove the duck from grill and place onto a cutting board for about 15 minutes before carving.
7. With a sharp knife, cut the duck into desired-sized pieces and serve.

Nutritional Information per Serving:

- Calories 878
- Total Fat 52.1 g
- Saturated Fat 13.9 g
- Cholesterol 3341 mg
- Sodium 2300 mg
- Total Carbs 45.4 g
- Fiber 0.7 g
- Sugar 39.6 g
- Protein 51 g

Sweet & Spicy Chicken Thighs

Preparation Time: 15 minutes
Cooking Time: 15 minutes
Servings: 4

Ingredients:

- 2 garlic cloves, minced
- ¼ cup honey
- 2 tablespoons soy sauce
- ¼ teaspoon red pepper flakes, crushed
- 4 (5-ounce) skinless, boneless chicken thighs
- 2 tablespoons olive oil
- 2 teaspoons sweet rub
- ¼ teaspoon red chili powder
- Ground black pepper, as required

Method:

1. Preheat the Wood Pellet Smoker and Grill on grill setting to 400 degrees F.
2. In a small bowl, add garlic, honey, soy sauce and red pepper flakes and with a wire whisk, beat until well combined.
3. Coat chicken thighs with oil and season with sweet rub, chili powder and black pepper generously.
4. Arrange the chicken drumsticks onto the grill and cook for about 15 minutes per
5. In the last 4-5 minutes of cooking, coat drumsticks with garlic mixture.
6. Serve immediately.

Nutritional Information per Serving:

- Calories 309
- Total Fat 12.1 g
- Saturated Fat 2.9 g
- Cholesterol 82 mg
- Sodium 504 mg
- Total Carbs 18.7 g
- Fiber 0.2 g
- Sugar 17.6 g
- Protein 32.3 g

Buttered Turkey

Preparation Time: 15 minutes
Cooking Time: 4 hours
Servings: 16

Ingredients:

- ½ pound butter, softened
- 2 tablespoons fresh thyme, chopped
- 2 fresh rosemary, chopped
- 6 garlic cloves, crushed
- 1 (20-pound) whole turkey, neck and giblets removed
- Salt and ground black pepper, as required

Method:

1. Preheat the Wood Pellet Smoker and Grill on smoke setting to 300 degrees F, using charcoal.
2. In a bowl, place butter, fresh herbs, garlic, salt and black pepper and mix well.
3. With your fingers, separate the turkey skin from breast to create a pocket.
4. Stuff the breast pocket with ¼-inch thick layer of butter mixture.
5. Season the turkey with salt and black pepper evenly.
6. Arrange the turkey onto the grill and cook for 3-4 hours.
7. Remove turkey from pallet grill and place onto a cutting board for about 15-20 minutes before carving.
8. With a sharp knife, cut the turkey into desired-sized pieces and serve.

Nutritional Information per Serving:

- Calories 965
- Total Fat 52 g
- Saturated Fat 19.9 g
- Cholesterol 385 mg
- Sodium 1916 mg
- Total Carbs 0.6 g
- Fiber 0.2 g
- Sugar 0 g
- Protein 106.5 g

Rosemary Cornish Hens

Preparation Time: 1 hour
Cooking Time: 15 minutes
Servings: 4

Ingredients:

- 4 Cornish game hens
- 4 fresh rosemary sprigs
- 4 tablespoons butter, melted
- 4 teaspoons chicken rub

Method:

1. Preheat the Wood Pellet Smoker and Grill on grill setting to 375 degrees F.
2. With paper towels, pat dry the hens.
3. Tuck the wings behind the backs and with kitchen strings, tie the legs together.
4. Coat the outside of each hen with melted butter and sprinkle with rub evenly.
5. Stuff the cavity of each hen with a rosemary sprig.
6. Place the hens onto the grill and cook for about 50-60 minutes.
7. Remove the hens from grill and place onto a platter for about 10 minutes.
8. Cut each hen into desired-sized pieces and serve.

Nutritional Information per Serving:

- Calories 430
- Total Fat 33 g
- Saturated Fat 13.4 g
- Cholesterol 183 mg
- Sodium 331 mg
- Total Carbs 2.1 g
- Fiber 0.7 g
- Sugar 0 g
- Protein 25.4 g

Bacon Wrapped Chicken Breasts

Preparation Time: 0 minute
Cooking Time: 3 hours
Servings: 6

Ingredients:

For Brine:

- ¼ cup brown sugar
- ¼ cup kosher salt
- 4 cups water

For Chicken:

- 6 skinless, boneless chicken breasts
- ¼ cup chicken rub
- 18 bacon slices
- 1½ cups BBQ sauce

Method:

1. For brine: in a large pitcher, dissolve sugar and salt in water.
2. Place the chicken breasts in brine and refrigerate for about 2 hours, flipping once in the middle way.
3. Preheat the Wood Pellet Smoker and Grill on grill setting to 230 degrees F.
4. Remove chicken breasts from brine and rinse under cold running water.
5. Season chicken breasts with rub generously.
6. Arrange 3 bacon strips of bacon onto a cutting board, against each other.
7. Place 1 chicken breast across the bacon, leaving enough bacon on the left side to wrap it over just a little.
8. Wrap the bacon strips around chicken breast and secure with toothpicks.
9. Repeat with remaining breasts and bacon slices.
10. Arrange the chicken breasts into pellet grill and cook for about 2½ hours.
11. Coat the breasts with BBQ sauce and cook for about 30 minutes more.
12. Serve immediately.

Nutritional Information per Serving:

- Calories 481
- Total Fat 12.3 g

- Saturated Fat 4.2 g
- Cholesterol 41 mg
- Sodium 3000 mg
- Total Carbs 32 g
- Fiber 0.4g
- Sugar 22.2 g
- Protein 55.9 g

Glazed Chicken Drumsticks

Preparation Time: 15 minutes
Cooking Time: 2 hours
Servings: 6

Ingredients:

- 1 cup fresh orange juice
- ¼ cup honey
- 2 tablespoons sweet chili sauce
- 2 tablespoons hoisin sauce
- 2 tablespoons fresh ginger, grated finely
- 2 tablespoons garlic, minced
- 1 teaspoon Sriracha
- ½ teaspoon sesame oil
- 6 chicken drumsticks

Method:

1. Preheat the Wood Pellet Smoker and Grill on smoke setting to 225 degrees F, using charcoal.
2. In a bowl, place all ingredients except for chicken drumsticks and mix until well combined.
3. Reserve half of honey mixture in a small bowl.
4. In the bowl of remaining sauce, add drumsticks and mix well.
5. Arrange the chicken drumsticks onto the grill and cook for about 2 hours, basting with remaining sauce occasionally.
6. Serve hot.

Nutritional Information per Serving:

- Calories 385
- Total Fat 10.5 g
- Saturated Fat 2.7 g
- Cholesterol 150 mg
- Sodium 270 mg
- Total Carbs 22.7 g
- Fiber 0.6 g
- Sugar 18.6 g
- Protein 47.6 g

Coffee Flavored Chicken

Preparation Time: 15 minutes
Cooking Time: 5 hours
Servings: 6

Ingredients:

- ¾ cup dark brown sugar
- ½ cup ground espresso beans
- 1 tablespoon ground cumin
- 1 tablespoon ground cinnamon
- 1 tablespoon garlic powder
- 1 tablespoon cayenne pepper
- Salt and ground black pepper, as required
- 1 (4-pound) whole chicken, neck and giblets removed

Method:

1. Preheat the Wood Pellet Smoker and Grill on grill setting to 200-225 degrees F.
2. In a bowl, mix together brown sugar, ground espresso, spices, salt and black pepper.
3. Rub the chicken with spice mixture generously.
4. Place the chicken onto the grill and cook for about 3-5 hours.
5. Remove chicken from grill and place onto a cutting board for about 10 minutes before carving.
6. With a sharp knife, cut the chicken into desired-sized pieces and serve.

Nutritional Information per Serving:

- Calories 540
- Total Fat 9.6 g
- Saturated Fat 2.6 g
- Cholesterol 233 mg
- Sodium 226mg
- Total Carbs 20.7 g
- Fiber 1.2 g
- Sugar 18.1 g
- Protein 88.3 g

Glazed Turkey Breast

Preparation Time: 15 minutes
Cooking Time: 4 hours
Servings: 6

Ingredients:

- ½ cup honey
- ¼ cup dry sherry
- 1 tablespoon butter
- 2 tablespoons fresh lemon juice
- Salt, as required
- 1 (3-3½-pound) skinless, boneless turkey breast

Method:

1. In a small pan, place honey, sherry and butter over low heat and cook until the mixture becomes smooth, stirring continuously.
2. Remove from heat and stir in lemon juice and salt. Set aside to cool.
3. Transfer the honey mixture and turkey breast in a sealable bag.
4. Seal the bag and shake to coat well.
5. Refrigerate for about 6-10 hours.
6. Preheat the Wood Pellet Smoker and Grill on grill setting to 225-250 degrees F.
7. Place the turkey breast onto the grill and cook for about 2½-4 hours or until desired doneness.
8. Remove turkey breast from pallet grill and place onto a cutting board for about 15-20 minutes before slicing.
9. With a sharp knife, cut the turkey breast into desired-sized slices and serve.

Nutritional Information per Serving:

- Calories 443
- Total Fat 11.4 g
- Saturated Fat 4.8 g
- Cholesterol 159 mg
- Sodium 138 mg
- Total Carbs 23.7 g
- Fiber 0.1 g
- Sugar 23.4 g

- Protein 59.2 g

Glazed Chicken Wings

Preparation Time: 15 minutes
Cooking Time: 2 hours
Servings: 6

Ingredients:

- 2 pounds chicken wings
- 2 garlic cloves, crushed
- 3 tablespoons hoisin sauce
- 2 tablespoons soy sauce
- 1 teaspoon dark sesame oil
- 1 tablespoon honey
- ½ teaspoon ginger powder
- 1 tablespoon sesame seeds, toasted lightly

Method:

1. Preheat the Wood Pellet Smoker and Grill on grill setting to 225 degrees F.
2. Arrange the wings onto the lower rack of grill and cook for about 1½ hours.
3. Meanwhile, in a large bowl, mix together remaining all ingredients.
4. Remove wings from grill and place in the bowl of garlic mixture.
5. Coat wings with garlic mixture generously.
6. Now, set the grill to 375 degrees F.
7. Arrange the coated wings onto a foil-lined baking sheet and sprinkle with sesame seeds.
8. Place the pan onto the lower rack of pellet grill and cook for about 25-30 minutes.
9. Serve immediately.

Nutritional Information per Serving:

- Calories 336
- Total Fat 13 g
- Saturated Fat 3.3 g
- Cholesterol 135 mg
- Sodium 560 mg
- Total Carbs 7.6 g
- Fiber 0.5 g
- Sugar 5.2 g
- Protein 44.7 g

Chicken Casserole

Preparation Time: 15 minutes
Cooking Time: 55 minutes
Servings: 8

Ingredients:

- 2 (15-ounce) cans cream of chicken soup
- 2 cups milk
- 2 tablespoons unsalted butter
- ¼ cup all-purpose flour
- 1 pound skinless, boneless chicken thighs, chopped
- ½ cup hatch chiles, chopped
- 2 medium onions, chopped
- 1 tablespoon fresh thyme, chopped
- Salt and ground black pepper, as required
- 1 cup cooked bacon, chopped
- 1 cup tater tots

Method:

1. Preheat the Wood Pellet Smoker and Grill on grill setting to 400 degrees F.
2. In a large bowl, mix together chicken soup and milk.
3. In a skillet, melt butter over medium heat.
4. Slowly, add flour and cook for about 1-2 minutes or until smooth, stirring continuously.
5. Slowly, add soup mixture, beating continuously until smooth.
6. Cook until mixture starts to thicken, stirring continuously.
7. Stir in remaining ingredients except bacon and simmer for about 10-15 minutes.
8. Stir in bacon and transfer mixture into a 2½-quart casserole dish.
9. Place tater tots on top of casserole evenly.
10. Arrange the pan onto the grill and cook for about 30-35 minutes.
11. Serve hot.

Nutritional Information per Serving:

- Calories 440
- Total Fat 25.8 g
- Saturated Fat 9.3 g

- Cholesterol 86 mg
- Sodium 1565 mg
- Total Carbs 22.2 g
- Fiber 1.5 g
- Sugar 4.6 g
- Protein 28.9 g

Chapter 4: Beef Recipes

Mustard Beef Short Ribs

Preparation Time: 15 minutes
Cooking Time: 3 hours
Servings: 6

Ingredients:

For Mustard Sauce:

- 1 cup prepared yellow mustard
- ¼ cup red wine vinegar
- ¼ cup dill pickle juice
- 2 tablespoons soy sauce
- 2 tablespoons Worcestershire sauce
- 1 teaspoon ground ginger
- 1 teaspoon granulated garlic

For Spice Rub:

- 2 tablespoons salt
- 2 tablespoons freshly ground black pepper
- 1 tablespoon white cane sugar
- 1 tablespoon granulated garlic

For Ribs:

- 6 (14-ounce) (4-5-inch long) beef short ribs

Method:

1. Preheat the Wood Pellet Smoker and Grill on smoke setting to 230-250 degrees F, using charcoal.
2. For sauce: in a bowl, mix together all ingredients.
3. For rub: in a small bowl, mix together all ingredients.
4. Coat the ribs with sauce generously and then sprinkle with spice rub evenly.
5. Place the ribs onto the grill over indirect heat, bone side down.
6. Cook for about 1-1½ hours.
7. Flip the side and cook for about 45 minutes.

8. Flip the side and cook for about 45 minutes more.
9. Remove the ribs from grill and place onto a cutting board for about 10 minutes before serving.
10. With a sharp knife, cut the ribs into equal sized individual pieces and serve.

Nutritional Information per Serving:

- Calories 867
- Total Fat 37.5 g
- Saturated Fat 13.7 g
- Cholesterol 361 mg
- Sodium 3462mg
- Total Carbs 7.7 g
- Fiber 2.1 g
- Sugar 3.6 g
- Protein 117.1 g

Brandy Beef Tenderloin

Preparation Time: 15 minutes
Cooking Time: 2 hours 2 minutes
Servings: 6

Ingredients:

For Brandy Butter:

- ½ cup butter
- 1 ounce brandy

For Brandy Sauce:

- 2 ounces brandy
- 8 garlic cloves, minced
- ¼ cup mixed fresh herbs (parsley, rosemary and thyme), chopped
- 2 teaspoons honey
- 2 teaspoons hot English mustard

For Tenderloin:

- 1 (2-pound) center-cut beef tenderloin
- Salt and cracked black peppercorns, as required

Method:

1. Preheat the Wood Pellet Smoker and Grill on grill setting to 230 degrees F.
2. For brandy butter: in a pan, melt butter over medium-low heat.
3. Stir in brandy and remove from heat.
4. Set aside, covered to keep warm.
5. For brandy sauce: in a bowl, add all ingredients and mix until well combined.
6. Season the tenderloin with salt and black peppercorns generously.
7. Coat tenderloin with brandy sauce evenly.
8. With a baster-injector, inject tenderloin with brandy butter.
9. Place the tenderloin onto the grill and cook for about ½-2 hours, injecting with brandy butter occasionally.
10. Remove the tenderloin from grill and place onto a cutting board for about 10-15 minutes before serving.
11. With a sharp knife, cut the tenderloin into desired-sized slices and serve.

Nutritional Information per Serving:

- Calories 496
- Total Fat 29.3 g
- Saturated Fat 15 g
- Cholesterol 180 mg
- Sodium 240 mg
- Total Carbs 4.4 g
- Fiber 0.7 g
- Sugar 2 g
- Protein 44.4 g

BBQ Meatloaf

Preparation Time: 20 minutes
Cooking Time: 2½ hours
Servings: 8

Ingredients:

For Meatloaf:

- 3 pounds ground beef
- 3 eggs
- ½ cup panko breadcrumbs
- 1 (10-ounce) can diced tomatoes with green chile peppers
- 1 large white onion, chopped
- 2 hot banana peppers, chopped
- 2 tablespoons seasoned salt
- 2 teaspoons liquid smoke flavoring
- 2 teaspoons smoked paprika
- 1 teaspoons onion salt
- 1 teaspoons garlic salt
- Salt and ground black pepper, as required

For Sauce:

- ½ cup ketchup
- ¼ cup tomato-based chile sauce
- ¼ cup white sugar
- 2 teaspoons Worcestershire sauce
- 2 teaspoons hot pepper sauce
- 1 teaspoon red pepper flakes, crushed
- 1 teaspoon red chili pepper
- Salt and ground black pepper, as required

Method:

1. Preheat the Wood Pellet Smoker and Grill on smoke setting to 225 degrees F, using charcoal.
2. Grease a loaf pan.

3. For meatloaf: in a bowl, add all ingredients and with your hands, mix until well combined.
4. Place the mixture into prepared loaf pan evenly.
5. Place the pan onto the grill and cook for about 2 hours.
6. For sauce: in a bowl, add all ingredients and beat until well combined.
7. Remove the pan from grill and drain excess grease from meatloaf.
8. Place sauce over meatloaf evenly and place the pan onto the grill.
9. Cook for about 30 minutes.
10. Remove the meatloaf from grill and set aside for about 10 minutes before serving.
11. Carefully, invert the meatloaf onto a platter.
12. Cut the meatloaf into desired-sized slices and serve.

Nutritional Information per Serving:

- Calories 423
- Total Fat 13 g
- Saturated Fat 4.7 g
- Cholesterol 213 mg
- Sodium 1879 mg
- Total Carbs 15.7 g
- Fiber 1.5 g
- Sugar 12.3 g
- Protein 54.9 g

Sweet & Spicy Beef Brisket

Preparation Time: 10 minutes
Cooking Time: 7 hours
Servings: 10

Ingredients:

- 1 cup paprika
- ¾ cup sugar
- 3 tablespoons garlic salt
- 3 tablespoons onion powder
- 1 tablespoon celery salt
- 1 tablespoon lemon pepper
- 1 tablespoon ground black pepper
- 1 teaspoon cayenne pepper
- 1 teaspoon mustard powder
- ½ teaspoon dried thyme, crushed
- 1 (5-6-pound) beef brisket, trimmed

Method:

1. In a bowl, place all ingredients except for beef brisket and mix well.
2. Rub the brisket with spice mixture generously.
3. With a plastic wrap, cover the brisket and refrigerate overnight.
4. Preheat the Wood Pellet Smoker and Grill on grill setting to 250 degrees F.
5. Place the brisket onto grill over indirect heat and cook for about 3-3½ hours.
6. Flip and cook for about 3-3½ hours more.
7. Remove the brisket from grill and place onto a cutting board for about 10-15 minutes before slicing.
8. With a sharp knife, cut the brisket in desired sized slices and serve.

Nutritional Information per Serving:

- Calories 536
- Total Fat 15.6 g
- Saturated Fat 5.6 g
- Cholesterol 203 mg
- Sodium 158 mg
- Total Carbs 24.8 g

- Fiber 4.5 g
- Sugar 17.4 g
- Protein 71.1 g

Herbed Prime Rib Roast

Preparation Time: 10 minutes
Cooking Time: 3 hours 50 minutes
Servings: 10

Ingredients:

- 1 (5-pound) prime rib roast
- Salt, as required
- 5 tablespoons olive oil
- 2 teaspoons dried thyme, crushed
- 2 teaspoons dried rosemary, crushed
- 2 teaspoons garlic powder
- 1 teaspoon onion powder
- 1 teaspoon paprika
- ½ teaspoon cayenne pepper
- Ground black pepper, as required

Method:

1. Season the roast with salt generously.
2. With a plastic wrap, cover the roast and refrigerate for about 24 hours.
3. In a bowl, mix together remaining ingredients and set aside for about 1 hour.
4. Rub the roast with oil mixture from both sides evenly.
5. Arrange the roast in a large baking sheet and refrigerate for about 6-12 hours.
6. Preheat the Wood Pellet Smoker and Grill on smoke setting to 225-230 degrees F, using pecan wood chips.
7. Place the roast onto the grill and cook for about 3-3½ hours.
8. Meanwhile, preheat the oven to 500 degrees F.
9. Remove the roast from grill and place onto a large baking sheet.
10. Place the baking sheet in oven and roast for about 15-20 minutes.
11. Remove the roast from oven and place onto a cutting board for about 10-15 minutes before serving.
12. With a sharp knife, cut the roast into desired-sized slices and serve.

Nutritional Information per Serving:

- Calories 605
- Total Fat 47.6 g

- Saturated Fat 17.2 g
- Cholesterol 135 mg
- Sodium 1285 mg
- Total Carbs 3.8 g
- Fiber 0.3 g
- Sugar0.3 g
- Protein 38 g

Beef Tenderloin

Preparation Time: 10 minutes
Cooking Time: 1 hour 19 minutes
Servings: 12

Ingredients:

- 1 (5-pound) beef tenderloin, trimmed
- Kosher salt, as required
- ¼ cup olive oil
- Freshly ground black pepper, as required

Method:

1. With kitchen strings, tie the tenderloin at 7-8 places.
2. Season tenderloin with kosher salt generously.
3. With a plastic wrap, cover the tenderloin and keep aside at room temperature for about 1 hour.
4. Preheat the Wood Pellet Smoker and Grill on grill setting to 225-250 degrees F.
5. Now, coat tenderloin with oil evenly and season with black pepper.
6. Arrange tenderloin onto the grill and cook for about 55-65 minutes.
7. Now, place cooking grate directly over hot coals and sear tenderloin for about 2 minutes per side.
8. Remove the tenderloin from the grill and place onto a cutting board for about 10-15 minutes before serving.
9. With a sharp knife, cut the tenderloin into desired-sized slices and serve.

Nutritional Information per Serving:

- Calories 425
- Total Fat 21.5 g
- Saturated Fat 7.2 g
- Cholesterol 174 mg
- Sodium 123 mg
- Total Carbs 0 g
- Fiber 0 g
- Sugar 0 g
- Protein 54.7 g

Beef Stuffed Bell Peppers

Preparation Time: 20 minutes
Cooking Time: 1 hour
Servings: 6

Ingredients:

- 6 large bell peppers
- 1 pound ground beef
- 1 small onion, chopped
- 2 garlic cloves, minced
- 2 cups cooked rice
- 1 cup frozen corn, thawed
- 1 cup cooked black beans
- 2/3 cup salsa
- 2 tablespoons Cajun rub
- 1½ cups Monterey Jack cheese, grated

Method:

1. Cut each bell pepper in half lengthwise through the stem.
2. Carefully, remove the seeds and ribs.
3. For stuffing: heat a large frying pan and cook the beef for about 6-7 minutes or until browned completely.
4. Add onion and garlic and cook for about 2-3 minutes.
5. Stir in remaining ingredients except cheese and cook for about 5 minutes.
6. Remove from the heat and set aside to cool slightly.
7. Preheat the Wood Pellet Smoker and Grill on grill setting to 350 degrees F.
8. Stuff each bell pepper half with stuffing mixture evenly.
9. Arrange the peppers onto grill, stuffing side up and cook for about 40 minutes.
10. Sprinkle each bell pepper half with cheese and cook for about 5 minutes more.
11. Remove the bell peppers from grill and serve hot.

Nutritional Information per Serving:

- Calories 675
- Total Fat 14.8 g
- Saturated Fat 7.5 g
- Cholesterol 93 mg

- Sodium 1167 mg
- Total Carbs 90.7 g
- Fiber 8.7 g
- Sugar 9.1 g
- Protein 43.9 g

Spicy Chuck Roast

Preparation Time: 10 minutes
Cooking Time: 4½ hours
Servings: 8

Ingredients:

- 2 tablespoons onion powder
- 2 tablespoons garlic powder
- 1 tablespoon red chili powder
- 1 tablespoon cayenne pepper
- Salt and ground black pepper, as required
- 1 (3 pound) beef chuck roast
- 16 fluid ounces warm beef broth

Method:

1. Preheat the Wood Pellet Smoker and Grill on grill setting to 250 degrees F.
2. In a bowl, mix together spices, salt and black pepper.
3. Rub the chuck roast with spice mixture evenly.
4. Place the rump roast onto the grill and cook for about 1½ hours per side.
5. Now, arrange chuck roast in a steaming pan with beef broth.
6. With a piece of foil, cover the pan and cook for about 2-3 hours.
7. Remove the chuck roast from grill and place onto a cutting board for about 20 minutes before slicing.
8. With a sharp knife, cut the chuck roast into desired-sized slices and serve.

Nutritional Information per Serving:

- Calories 645
- Total Fat 48 g
- Saturated Fat 19 g
- Cholesterol 175 mg
- Sodium 329 mg
- Total Carbs 4.2 g
- Fiber 1 g
- Sugar 1.4 g
- Protein 46.4 g

BBQ Spiced Flank Steak

Preparation Time: 15 minutes
Cooking Time: 30 minutes
Servings: 6

Ingredients:

- 1 (2-pound) beef flank steak
- 2 tablespoons olive oil
- ¼ cup BBQ rub
- 3 tablespoons blue cheese, crumbled
- 2 tablespoons butter, softened
- 1 teaspoon fresh chives, minced

Method:

1. Preheat the Wood Pellet Smoker and Grill on grill setting to 225 degrees F.
2. Coat the steak with oil evenly and season with BBQ rub.
3. Place the steak onto the grill and cook for about 10-15 minutes per side.
4. Remove the steak from grill and place onto a cutting board for about 10 minutes before slicing.
5. Meanwhile, in a bowl, add blue cheese, butter and chives and mix well.
6. With a sharp knife, cut the steak into thin strips across the grain.
7. Top with cheese mixture and serve.

Nutritional Information per Serving:

- Calories 370
- Total Fat 19.1 g
- Saturated Fat 7.5 g
- Cholesterol 148 mg
- Sodium 1666 mg
- Total Carbs 0.1 g
- Fiber 0 g
- Sugar 0 g
- Protein 46.8 g

Beef Rump Roast

Preparation Time: 10 minutes
Cooking Time: 6 hours
Servings: 8

Ingredients:

- 1 teaspoon smoked paprika
- 1 teaspoon cayenne pepper
- 1 teaspoon onion powder
- 1 teaspoon garlic powder
- Salt and ground black pepper, as required
- 3 pounds beef rump roast
- ¼ cup Worcestershire sauce

Method:

1. Preheat the Wood Pellet Smoker and Grill on smoke setting to 200 degrees F, using charcoal.
2. In a bowl, mix together all spices.
3. Coat the rump roast with Worcestershire sauce evenly and then, rub with spice mixture generously.
4. Place the rump roast onto the grill and cook for about 5-6 hours.
5. Remove the roast from the grill and place onto a cutting board for about 10-15 minutes before serving.
6. With a sharp knife, cut the roast into desired-sized slices and serve.

Nutritional Information per Serving:

- Calories 252
- Total Fat 9.1 g
- Saturated Fat 3 g
- Cholesterol 113 mg
- Sodium 200 mg
- Total Carbs 2.3 g
- Fiber 0.2 g
- Sugar 1.8 g
- Protein 37.8 g

Chapter 5: Pork Recipes

Glazed Pork Rack of Ribs

Preparation Time: 20 minutes
Cooking Time: 1 hour 55 minutes
Servings: 6

Ingredients:

- 2 bone-in racks of pork ribs, silver skin removed
- 6 ounces BBQ rub
- 8 ounces apple juice
- ½ cup BBQ sauce

Method:

1. Coat each rack of ribs with BBQ rub generously.
2. Arrange the racks onto a platter and set aside for about 30 minutes.
3. Preheat the Wood Pellet Smoker and Grill on grill setting to 225 degrees F.
4. Arrange the racks onto the grill, bone side down and cook for about 1 hour.
5. In a food-safe spray bottle, place apple juice.
6. Spray the racks with vinegar mixture evenly.
7. Cook for about 3½ hours, spraying with vinegar mixture after every 45 minutes.
8. Now, coat the racks with a thin layer of BBQ sauce evenly and cook for about 10 minutes more.
9. Remove the racks from grill and place onto a cutting board for about 10-15 minutes before slicing.
10. With a sharp knife, cut each rack into individual ribs and serve.

Nutritional Information per Serving:

- Calories 801
- Total Fat 406 g
- Saturated Fat 14.4 g
- Cholesterol 234 mg
- Sodium 558 mg
- Total Carbs 44.9 g
- Fiber 0.8 g
- Sugar 37.4 g

- Protein 60.4 g

Sweet & Spicy Pork Ribs

Preparation Time: 15 minutes
Cooking Time: 5 hours
Servings: 16

Ingredients:

- ¼ cup yellow honey mustard
- ¼ cup brown sugar
- 1/3 cup paprika
- ¼ cup garlic powder
- ¼ cup onion powder
- 2 tablespoons chipotle chili pepper flakes
- 1 tablespoon ground cumin
- Salt and ground black pepper, as required
- 2 tablespoons dried parsley flakes
- 8 pounds pork baby back ribs, silver skin removed

Method:

1. In a bowl, add all ingredients except for ribs and mix well.
2. Rub the pork ribs with spice mixture generously.
3. Preheat the Wood Pellet Smoker and Grill on smoke setting to 200 degrees F, using charcoal.
4. Arrange the ribs onto the grill and cook for about 2 hours.
5. Remove the ribs from grill and wrap in heavy duty foil.
6. Cook for about 2 hours.
7. Remove the foil and cook for about 1 hour more.
8. Remove the ribs from grill and place onto a cutting board for about 10-15 minutes before serving.

Nutritional Information per Serving:

- Calories 659
- Total Fat 40.7 g
- Saturated Fat 14.4 g
- Cholesterol 234 mg
- Sodium 186 mg
- Total Carbs 7.8 g

- Fiber 1.5 g
- Sugar 4.4 g
- Protein 61.1 g

Sweet & Spicy Pork Chops

Preparation Time: 10 minutes
Cooking Time: 1 hour 10 minutes
Servings: 4

Ingredients:

- 2 tablespoons dried thyme, crushed
- 2 tablespoons dark brown sugar
- 1 tablespoon cayenne pepper
- 1 tablespoon onion powder
- 1 tablespoon garlic powder
- 4 bone-in, center cut pork chops

Method:

1. In a bowl, place all ingredients except for pork chops and mix well.
2. Rub the pork chops with spice mixture generously.
3. With a plastic wrap, cover the pork chops and refrigerate overnight.
4. Preheat the Wood Pellet Smoker and Grill on smoke setting to 275 degrees F, using charcoal and soaked apple wood chips.
5. Place the chops onto the grill and cook for about 70 minutes.
6. Remove the chops from grill and place onto a platter for about 5 minutes before serving.

Nutritional Information per Serving:

- Calories 582
- Total Fat 42.6 g
- Saturated Fat 15.9 g
- Cholesterol 146 mg
- Sodium 123 mg
- Total Carbs 9 g
- Fiber 1.2 g
- Sugar 5.7 g
- Protein 39 g

Spiced Pork Butt Roast

Preparation Time: 10 minutes
Cooking Time: 14 hours
Servings: 14

Ingredients:

- ¼ cup brown sugar
- 2 tablespoons New Mexico chile powder
- 2 tablespoons garlic powder
- Salt, as required
- 1 (7-pound) fresh pork butt roast

Method:

1. Preheat the Wood Pellet Smoker and Grill on grill setting to 200-225 degrees F.
2. In a bowl, place all ingredients except for pork roast and mix well.
3. Rub the pork roast with spice mixture generously.
4. Arrange a roasting rack in a drip pan.
5. Place the pork roast onto the rack in drip pan.
6. Place the drip pan onto the grill and cook for about 8-14 hours or until desired doneness.
7. Remove the roast from grill and place onto a cutting board for about 10-15 minutes before slicing.
8. With a sharp knife, cut the roast into desired-sized slices and serve.

Nutritional Information per Serving:

- Calories 439
- Total Fat 28.3 g
- Saturated Fat 10.1 g
- Cholesterol 141 mg
- Sodium 164 mg
- Total Carbs 4 g
- Fiber 0.5 g
- Sugar 2.9 g
- Protein 40.5 g

Sweet & Spiced Glazed Ham

Preparation Time: 20 minutes
Cooking Time: 6 hours 5 minutes
Servings: 14

Ingredients:

For Rub Mixture:

- 1 tablespoon sugar
- 1 teaspoon mustard powder
- 1 tablespoon paprika
- ½ teaspoon cayenne pepper
- Ground black pepper, as required
- Salt, as required

For Ham:

- 1 (6-pound) ready-to-eat ham

For Sauce:

- ¾ cup chicken broth
- ¾ cup pineapple juice
- 2 tablespoons olive oil
- ½ teaspoon ground cloves
- ½ teaspoon mustard powder

For Glaze:

- ½ cup honey
- ¼ cup pineapple juice
- ½ teaspoon mustard powder
- Pinch of ground cloves

Method:

1. For rub mixture: in a bowl, mix together all ingredients.
2. Rub the ham with rub mixture generously.
3. With a piece of foil, cover the ham and refrigerate overnight.

4. Remove the ham from refrigerator and set aside in room temperature for about 1 hour.
5. Preheat the Wood Pellet Smoker and Grill on smoke setting to 210 degrees F, using charcoal.
6. Meanwhile, for sauce in a pan, place all ingredients over medium heat and cook until the sauce becomes warm enough, stirring continuously.
7. Place the ham onto grill and cook for about 6 hours, coating with sauce after every 1 hour.
8. Meanwhile, for glaze: in a bowl, mix together all ingredients.
9. During last 1 hour of cooking, coat the ham with glaze twice generously.
10. Remove the ham from grill and place onto a cutting board for about 20-25 minutes before serving.
11. With a sharp knife, cut the ham into desired-sized slices and serve.

Nutritional Information per Serving:

- Calories 389
- Total Fat 19 g
- Saturated Fat 6 g
- Cholesterol 111 mg
- Sodium 2500 mg
- Total Carbs 21.1 g
- Fiber 2.9 g
- Sugar 12.7 g
- Protein 32.8 g

Simple Pork Belly

Preparation Time: 10 minutes
Cooking Time: 8 hours
Servings: 12

Ingredients:

- 1 (5-pound) pork belly, skin removed
- Kosher salt and coarsely ground black pepper, as required

Method:

1. Preheat the Wood Pellet Smoker and Grill on smoke setting to 225 degrees F, using charcoal.
2. Rub the pork belly with salt and black pepper generously.
3. Arrange the pork belly onto the grill and cook for about 6-8 hours,
4. Remove the pork belly from grill and place onto a cutting board for about 10-15 minutes before slicing.
5. With a sharp knife, cut the pork belly into desired-sized slices and serve.

Nutritional Information per Serving:

- Calories 534
- Total Fat 46.7 g
- Saturated Fat 15.6 g
- Cholesterol 100 mg
- Sodium 790 mg
- Total Carbs 0 g
- Fiber 0 g
- Sugar 0 g
- Protein 28.9 g

BBQ Rub Pork Chops

Preparation Time: 15 minutes
Cooking Time: 1 hour 35 minutes
Servings: 4

Ingredients:

For Brine:

- 8 cups apple juice
- 1 cup light brown sugar
- ½ cup kosher salt
- ½ cup BBQ rub

For Pork Chops:

- 4 thick cut pork loin chops
- 2 tablespoons BBQ rub
- 1 tablespoon Montreal steak seasoning

Method:

1. For brine: in a large pan, add 4 cups of apple juice and cook until heated completely.
2. Add sugar, salt and dry rub and cook until dissolved, stirring continuously.
3. Remove the pan from heat and stir in remaining apple juice.
4. Set aside to cool completely.
5. In a larger zip lock, add brine mixture and chops.
6. Seal the bag and refrigerate for about 2 hours.
7. Preheat the Wood Pellet Smoker and Grill on grill setting to 250 degrees F.
8. Remove the chops from brine and set aside for about 10-15 minutes.
9. Now, season the chops with BBQ rub and steak seasoning evenly.
10. Place the chops onto the grill and cook for about 1½ hours.
11. Remove the chops from grill and keep aside for about 5 minutes before serving.

Nutritional Information per Serving:

- Calories 609
- Total Fat 12.6 g
- Saturated Fat 4.2 g
- Cholesterol 85 mg

- Sodium 20000 mg
- Total Carbs 92.6 g
- Fiber 1 g
- Sugar84.2 g
- Protein 29.5 g

Jam Glazed Sausage

Preparation Time: 15 minutes
Cooking Time: 23 minutes
Servings: 6

Ingredients:

- ½ cup apricot jam
- 1 tablespoon Dijon mustard
- 12 breakfast sausage links

Method:

1. Preheat the Wood Pellet Smoker and Grill on grill setting to 350 degrees F.
2. In a small pan, add jam and mustard over medium-low heat and cook until warmed.
3. Reduce the heat to low to keep the glaze warm.
4. Arrange the sausage links onto grill and cook for about 10-15 minutes, flipping twice.
5. Coat the sausage links with jam glaze evenly and cook for about 2-3 minutes.
6. Remove the sausage links from grill and serve alongside the remaining glaze.

Nutritional Information per Serving:

- Calories 575
- Total Fat 42.7 g
- Saturated Fat 13.7 g
- Cholesterol 126 mg
- Sodium 1164 mg
- Total Carbs 17.3 g
- Fiber 0.2 g
- Sugar 11.6 g
- Protein 29.5 g

Glazed Pork Tenderloin

Preparation Time: 10 minutes
Cooking Time: 3 hours
Servings: 6

Ingredients:

- ½ cup apple cider
- 3 tablespoons honey
- 2 (1¼-1½-pound) pork tenderloins, silver skin removed
- 3 tablespoons sweet rub

Method:

1. In a small bowl, mix together apple cider and honey.
2. Coat the outside of tenderloins with honey mixture and season with the rub generously.
3. With a plastic wrap, cover each tenderloin and refrigerate for about 2-3 hours.
4. Preheat the Wood Pellet Smoker and Grill on grill setting to 225 degrees F.
5. Arrange the tenderloins onto the grill and cook for about 2½-3 hours.
6. Remove the pork tenderloins from grill and place onto a cutting board for about 5 minutes before slicing.
7. With a sharp knife, cut each pork tenderloin into desired-sized slices and serve.

Nutritional Information per Serving:

- Calories 498
- Total Fat 18.4 g
- Saturated Fat 6.7g
- Cholesterol 213 mg
- Sodium 146 mg
- Total Carbs 11.1 g
- Fiber 0 g
- Sugar 10.9 g
- Protein 67.8 g

Honey Glazed ham

Preparation Time: 15 minutes
Cooking Time: 1 hour 20 minutes
Servings: 16

Ingredients:

- 1 cup honey
- ¼ cup dark corn syrup
- 1 (7-pound) ready-to-eat ham
- ¼ cup whole cloves
- ½ cup butter, softened

Method:

1. Preheat the Wood Pellet Smoker and Grill on grill setting to 325 degrees F, using charcoal.
2. In a small pan, add honey and corn syrup and cook until heated slightly, stirring continuously.
3. Remove the pan of glaze from heat and set aside.
4. With a sharp knife, score the ham in a cross pattern.
5. Insert whole cloves at the crossings.
6. Coat the ham with butter evenly.
7. Arrange ham in foil lined roasting pan and top with ¾ of glaze evenly.
8. Arrange the pan onto the grill and cook for about 1¼ hours, coating with remain glaze after every 10-15 minutes.
9. Remove the ham from grill and place onto a cutting board for about 20-25 minutes before serving.
10. With a sharp knife, cut the ham into desired-sized slices and serve.

Nutritional Information per Serving:

- Calories 457
- Total Fat 23.1 g
- Saturated Fat 9.6 g
- Cholesterol 128 mg
- Sodium 2633 mg
- Total Carbs 29.7 g
- Fiber 3.2 g

- Sugar 18.7 g
- Protein 33.2 g

Chapter 6: Lamb Recipes

Herbed Rack of Lamb

Preparation Time: 15 minutes
Cooking Time: 2 hours
Servings: 3

Ingredients:

- 2 tablespoons fresh sage
- 2 tablespoons fresh rosemary
- 2 tablespoons fresh thyme
- 2 garlic cloves, peeled
- 1 tablespoon honey
- Salt and ground black pepper, as required
- ¼ cup olive oil
- 1 (1½-pound) rack of lamb, trimmed

Method:

1. In a food processor, add all ingredients except for oil and rack of lamb rack and pulse until well combined.
2. While motor is running, slowly add oil and pulse until a smooth paste is formed.
3. Coat the rib rack with paste generously and refrigerate for about 2 hours.
4. Preheat the Wood Pellet Smoker and Grill on grill setting to 225 degrees F.
5. Arrange the rack of lamb onto the grill and cook for about 2 hours.
6. Remove the rack of lamb from grill and place onto a cutting board for about 10-15 minutes before slicing.
7. With a sharp knife, cut the rack into individual ribs and serve.

Nutritional Information per Serving:

- Calories 566
- Total Fat 37.5 g
- Saturated Fat 9.7 g
- Cholesterol 151 mg
- Sodium 214 mg
- Total Carbs 9.8 g
- Fiber 2.2 g

- Sugar 5.8g
- Protein 46.7 g

Stuffed Leg of Lamb

Preparation Time: 20 minutes
Cooking Time: 2½ hours
Servings: 8

Ingredients:

For Filling:

- 1 (8-ounce) package cream cheese, softened
- ¼ cup cooked bacon, crumbled
- 1 jalapeño pepper, seeded and chopped

For Spice Mixture:

- 1 tablespoon dried rosemary, crushed
- 2 teaspoons garlic powder
- 1 teaspoon onion powder
- 1 teaspoon paprika
- 1 teaspoon cayenne pepper
- Salt, as required

For Leg of Lamb:

- 1 (4-5-pound) leg of lamb, butterflied
- 2-3 tablespoons olive oil

Method:

1. Preheat the Wood Pellet Smoker and Grill on smoke setting to 225-240 degrees F, using charcoal and cherry wood chips.
2. For filling: in a bowl, add all ingredients and mix until well combined.
3. For spice mixture: in another small bowl, mix together all ingredients.
4. Place the leg of lamb onto a smooth surface.
5. Sprinkle the inside of leg with some spice mixture.
6. Place filling mixture over the inside surface evenly.
7. Roll the leg of lamb tightly and with a butcher's twine, tie the roll to secure the filling
8. Coat the outer side of roll with olive oil evenly and then sprinkle with spice mixture.
9. Arrange the leg of lamb onto the grill and cook for about 2-2½ hours.

10. Remove the leg of lamb from grill and place onto a cutting board.
11. With a piece of foil cover the leg of lamb loosely for about 20-25 minutes before serving.
12. With a sharp knife, cut the leg of lamb into desired-sized slices and serve.

Nutritional Information per Serving:

- Calories 700
- Total Fat 37.2 g
- Saturated Fat 15.2 g
- Cholesterol 294 mg
- Sodium 478 mg
- Total Carbs 2.2 g
- Fiber 0.5 g
- Sugar 0.5 g
- Protein 84.6 g

Simple Lamb Chops

Preparation Time: 10 minutes
Cooking Time: 12 minutes
Servings: 6

Ingredients:

- 6 (6-ounce) lamb chops
- 3 tablespoons olive oil
- Salt and ground black pepper, as required

Method:

1. Preheat the Wood Pellet Smoker and Grill on grill setting to 450 degrees F.
2. Coat the lamb chops with oil and then, season with salt and black pepper evenly.
3. Arrange the chops onto the grill and cook for about 4-6 minutes per side.
4. Remove the chops from grill and serve hot.

Nutritional Information per Serving:

- Calories 376
- Total Fat 19.5 g
- Saturated Fat 5.5 g
- Cholesterol 153 mg
- Sodium 156 mg
- Total Carbs 0 g
- Fiber 0 g
- Sugar 0 g
- Protein 47.8 g

Cheesy Lamb Burgers

Preparation Time: 10 minutes
Cooking Time: 18 minutes
Servings: 4

Ingredients:

- 2 pounds ground lamb
- 1 cup Parmigiano-Reggiano cheese, grated
- Salt and ground black pepper, as required

Method:

1. Preheat the Wood Pellet Smoker and Grill on grill setting to 425 degrees F.
2. In a bowl, add all ingredients and mix until well combined.
3. Make 4 (¾-inch thick) patties from mixture.
4. With your thumbs, make a shallow but wide depression in each patty.
5. Arrange the patties onto the grill, depression-side down and cook for about 8 minutes.
6. Flip the patties and cook for about 8-10 minutes.
7. Remove the patties from grill and serve immediately.

Nutritional Information per Serving:

- Calories 502
- Total Fat 22.6 g
- Saturated Fat 9.9 g
- Cholesterol 220 mg
- Sodium 331 mg
- Total Carbs 0 g
- Fiber 0 g
- Sugar 0 g
- Protein 71.7 g

Cola Flavored Rack of Lamb

Preparation Time: 15 minutes
Cooking Time: 3 hours
Servings: 12

Ingredients:

- 4 (1½-pound) racks of lamb, trimmed
- 1 tablespoon unsweetened cocoa powder
- 1 tablespoon brown sugar
- 1 tablespoon smoked paprika
- Salt and ground black pepper, as required
- 1 cup cherry cola

Method:

1. Preheat the Wood Pellet Smoker and Grill on grill setting to 225 degrees F.
2. With a sharp knife, make ½x¼-inch cuts in each rack of lamb.
3. In a bowl, place remaining ingredients except for cherry cola and mix until well combined.
4. Rub the racks with sugar mixture generously.
5. Arrange the racks onto the grill and cook for about 2½-3 hours, coating with cherry cola after every 1 hour.
6. Remove the racks from grill and place onto a cutting board for about 10-15 minutes before slicing.
7. With a sharp knife, cut each rack of lamb into individual ribs and serve.

Nutritional Information per Serving:

- Calories 437
- Total Fat 16.8g
- Saturated Fat 6 g
- Cholesterol 204 mg
- Sodium 186 mg
- Total Carbs 3.6 g
- Fiber 0.4 g
- Sugar 2.7 g
- Protein 63.9 g

Wine Flavored Leg of Lamb

Preparation Time: 15 minutes
Cooking Time: 5 hours
Servings: 8

Ingredients:

- ½ cup olive oil
- ½ cup red wine vinegar
- ½ cup dry white wine
- 1 tablespoon garlic, minced
- 1 teaspoon dried marjoram, crushed
- 1 teaspoon dried rosemary, crushed
- Salt and ground black pepper, as required
- 1 (5-pound) leg of lamb

Method:

1. In a bowl, add all ingredients except for leg of lamb and mix until well combined.
2. In a large resealable bag, add marinade and leg of lamb.
3. Seal the bag and shake to coat completely.
4. Refrigerate for about 4-6 hours, flipping occasionally.
5. Preheat the Wood Pellet Smoker and Grill on grill setting to 225 degrees F.
6. Arrange the leg of lamb onto the grill and cook for about 4-5 hours.
7. Remove the leg of lamb from grill and place onto a cutting board for about 20 minutes before slicing.
8. With a sharp knife, cut the leg of lamb into desired-sized slices and serve.

Nutritional Information per Serving:

- Calories 653
- Total Fat 33.4 g
- Saturated Fat 9.2 g
- Cholesterol 255 mg
- Sodium 237 mg
- Total Carbs 1 g
- Fiber 0.1 g
- Sugar 0.2 g
- Protein 79.7 g

Buttermilk Brined Shoulder Chops

Preparation Time: 15 minutes
Cooking Time: 30 minutes
Servings: 4

Ingredients:

- 4 lamb shoulder chops
- 4 cups buttermilk
- 1 cup cold water
- ¼ cup kosher salt
- 2 tablespoons olive oil
- 1 tablespoon Texas style rub

Method:

1. In a large bowl, add buttermilk, water and salt and stir until salt is dissolved.
2. Add chops and coat with mixture evenly.
3. Refrigerate for at least 4 hours.
4. Remove the chops from bowl and rinse under cold running water.
5. Coat the chops with olive oil and then sprinkle with rub evenly.
6. Preheat the Wood Pellet Smoker and Grill on smoke setting to 240 degrees F, using charcoal.
7. Arrange the chops onto grill and cook for about 25-30 minute or until desired doneness.
8. Meanwhile preheat the broiler of oven. Grease a broiler pan.
9. Remove the chops from grill and place onto the prepared broiler pan.
10. Transfer the broiler pan into the oven and broil for about 3-5 minutes or until browned.
11. Remove the chops from oven and serve hot.

Nutritional Information per Serving:

- Calories 414
- Total Fat 22.7 g
- Saturated Fat 6.9 g
- Cholesterol 123 mg
- Sodium 7000 mg
- Total Carbs 11.7 g

- Fiber 0 g
- Sugar 11.7 g
- Protein 41.2 g

Seasoned Lamb Shoulder

Preparation Time: 15 minutes
Cooking Time: 5¾ hours
Servings: 6

Ingredients:

- 1 (5-pound) bone-in lamb shoulder, trimmed
- 3-4 tablespoons Moroccan seasoning
- 2 tablespoons olive oil
- 1 cup water
- ¼ cup apple cider vinegar

Method:

1. Preheat the Wood Pellet Smoker and Grill on smoke setting to 275 degrees F, using charcoal.
2. Coat the lamb shoulder with oil evenly and then rub with Moroccan seasoning generously.
3. Place the lamb shoulder onto the grill and cook for about 45 minutes.
4. In a food-safe spray bottle, mix together vinegar and water.
5. Spray the lamb shoulder with vinegar mixture evenly.
6. Cook for about 4-5 hours, spraying with vinegar mixture after every 20 minutes.
7. Remove the lamb shoulder from grill and place onto a cutting board for about 20 minutes before slicing.
8. With a sharp knife, cut the lamb shoulder in desired sized slices and serve.

Nutritional Information per Serving:

- Calories 563
- Total Fat 25.2 g
- Saturated Fat 7.5 g
- Cholesterol 251 mg
- Sodium 1192 mg
- Total Carbs 3.1 g
- Fiber 0 g
- Sugar 1.4 g
- Protein 77.4 g

Sweet & Tangy Braised Lamb Shank

Preparation Time: 15 minutes
Cooking Time: 10 hours
Servings: 2

Ingredients:

- 2 (1¼-pound) lamb shanks
- 1-2 cups water
- ¼ cup brown sugar
- 1/3 cup rice wine
- 1/3 cup soy sauce
- 1 tablespoon dark sesame oil
- 4 (1½x½-inch) orange zest strips
- 2 (3-inch long) cinnamon sticks
- 1½ teaspoons Chinese five spice powder

Method:

1. Preheat the Wood Pellet Smoker and Grill on smoke setting to 225-250 degrees F, using charcoal and soaked apple wood chips.
2. With a sharp knife, pierce each lamb shank at many places.
3. In a bowl, add remaining all ingredients and mix until sugar is dissolved.
4. In a large foil pan, place the lamb shanks and top with sugar mixture evenly.
5. Place the foil pan onto the grill and cook for about 8-10 hours, flipping after every 30 minutes. (If required, add enough water to keep the liquid ½-inch over).
6. Remove from the grill and serve hot.

Nutritional Information per Serving:

- Calories 1200
- Total Fat 48.4 g
- Saturated Fat 15.8 g
- Cholesterol 510 mg
- Sodium 2000 mg
- Total Carbs 39.7 g
- Fiber 0.3 g
- Sugar 29 g
- Protein 161.9 g

Lemony & Spicy Lamb Shoulder

Preparation Time: 15 minutes
Cooking Time: 2½ hours
Servings: 8

Ingredients:

- 1 (5-pound) bone-in lamb shoulder, trimmed
- 2 tablespoons olive oil
- 1 tablespoon fresh lemon juice
- 1 tablespoon fresh ginger, peeled
- 4-6 garlic cloves, peeled
- ½ tablespoon ground cumin
- ½ tablespoon paprika
- ½ tablespoon ground turmeric
- ½ tablespoon ground allspice
- Salt and ground black pepper, as required

Method:

1. With a sharp knife, score the skin of the lamb shoulder into diamond pattern.
2. In a food processor, add remaining all ingredients and pule until smooth.
3. Coat the lamb shoulder with pureed mixture generously.
4. Arrange the lamb shoulder into a large baking dish and refrigerate, covered overnight.
5. Remove the baking dish of shoulder from refrigerator and set aside at room temperature for at least 1 hour before cooking.
6. Preheat the Wood Pellet Smoker and Grill on grill setting to 225 degrees F.
7. Place the lamb shoulder onto the grill and cook for about 2½ hours.
8. Remove the lamb shoulder from grill and place onto a cutting board for about 20 minutes before slicing.
9. With a sharp knife, cut the lamb shoulder into desired-sized slices and serve.

Nutritional Information per Serving:

- Calories 417
- Total Fat 18.8 g
- Saturated Fat 5.6 g
- Cholesterol 188 mg

- Sodium 222 mg
- Total Carbs 2 g
- Fiber 0.5 g
- Sugar 0.1 g
- Protein 58.1 g

Chapter 7: Fish & Seafood Recipes

Rosemary Trout

Preparation Time: 10 minutes
Cooking Time: 5 hours
Servings: 8

Ingredients:

- 1 (7-pound) whole lake trout, butterflied
- ½ cup kosher salt
- ½ cup fresh rosemary, chopped
- 2 teaspoons lemon zest, grated finely

Method:

1. Rub the trout with salt generously and then, sprinkle with rosemary and lemon zest.
2. Arrange the trout in a large baking dish and refrigerate for about 7-8 hours.
3. Remove the trout from baking dish and rinse under cold running water to remove the salt.
4. With paper towels, pat dry the trout completely.
5. Arrange a wire rack in a sheet pan.
6. Place the trout onto the wire rack, skin side down and refrigerate for about 24 hours.
7. Preheat the Wood Pellet Smoker and Grill on grill setting to 180 degrees F, using charcoal.
8. Place the trout onto the grill and cook for about 2-4 hours or until desired doneness.
9. Remove the trout from grill and place onto a cutting board for about 5 minurtes before serving.

Nutritional Information per Serving:

- Calories 633
- Total Fat 31.8 g
- Saturated Fat 7.9 g
- Cholesterol 153 mg
- Sodium 5000 mg

- Total Carbs 2.4 g
- Fiber 1.6 g
- Sugar 0 g
- Protein 85.2 g

Prosciutto Wrapped Scallops

Preparation Time: 15 minutes
Cooking Time: 40 minutes
Servings: 4

Ingredients:

- 8 large scallops, shelled and cleaned
- 8 extra-thin prosciutto slices

Method:

1. Preheat the Wood Pellet Smoker and Grill on grill setting to 225-250 degrees F.
2. Arrange the prosciutto slices onto a smooth surface.
3. Place 1 scallop on the edge of 1 prosciutto slice and roll it up tucking in the sides of the prosciutto to cover completely.
4. Repeat with remaining scallops and prosciutto slices
5. Arrange the wrapped scallops onto a small wire rack.
6. Place the wire rack onto the grill and cook for about 40 minutes.
7. Remove the scallops from grill and serve hot.

Nutritional Information per Serving:

- Calories 160
- Total Fat 6.7 g
- Saturated Fat 2.3 g
- Cholesterol 64 mg
- Sodium 1000 mg
- Total Carbs 1.4 g
- Fiber 0 g
- Sugar 0 g
- Protein 23.5 g

Lemony Lobster Tails

Preparation Time: 15 minutes
Cooking Time: 25 hours
Servings: 4

Ingredients:

- ½ cup butter, melted
- 2 garlic cloves, minced
- 2 teaspoons fresh lemon juice
- Salt and ground black pepper, as required
- 4 (8-ounce) lobster tails

Method:

1. Preheat the Wood Pellet Smoker and Grill on grill setting to 450 degrees F.
2. In a metal pan, add all ingredients except for lobster tails and mix well.
3. Place the pan onto the grill and cook for about 10 minutes.
4. Meanwhile, cut down the top of the shell and expose lobster meat.
5. Remove pan of butter mixture rom grill.
6. Coat the lobster meat with butter mixture.
7. Place the lobster tails onto the grill and cook for about 15 minutes, coating with butter mixture once halfway through.
8. Remove from the grill and serve hot.

Nutritional Information per Serving:

- Calories 409
- Total Fat 24.9 g
- Saturated Fat 15.1 g
- Cholesterol 392 mg
- Sodium 1305 mg
- Total Carbs 0.6 g
- Fiber 0 g
- Sugar 0.1 g
- Protein 43.5 g

Simple Mahi-Mahi

Preparation Time: 10 minutes
Cooking Time: 10 minutes
Servings: 4

Ingredients:

- 4 (6-ounce) mahi-mahi fillets
- 2 tablespoons olive oil
- Salt and ground black pepper, as required

Method:

1. Preheat the Wood Pellet Smoker and Grill on grill setting to 350 degrees F.
2. Coat fish fillets with olive oil and season with salt and black pepper evenly.
3. Place the fish fillets onto the grill and cook for about 5 minutes per side.
4. Remove the fish fillets from grill and serve hot.

Nutritional Information per Serving:

- Calories 195
- Total Fat 7 g
- Saturated Fat 1 g
- Cholesterol 60 mg
- Sodium 182 mg
- Total Carbs 0 g
- Fiber 0 g
- Sugar 0 g
- Protein 31.6g

Wine Brined Salmon

Preparation Time: 15 minutes
Cooking Time: 5 hours
Servings: 4

Ingredients:

- 2 cups low-sodium soy sauce
- 1 cup dry white wine
- 1 cup water
- ½ teaspoon Tabasco sauce
- 1/3 cup sugar
- ¼ cup salt
- ½ teaspoon garlic powder
- ½ teaspoon onion powder
- Ground black pepper, as required
- 4 (6-ounce) salmon fillets

Method:

1. In a large bowl, add all ingredients except salmon and stir until sugar is dissolved.
2. Add salmon fillets and coat with brine well.
3. Refrigerate, covered overnight.
4. Remove salmon from bowl and rinse under cold running water.
5. With paper towels, pat dry the salmon fillets.
6. Arrange a wire rack in a sheet pan.
7. Place the salmon fillets onto wire rack, skin side down and set aside to cool for about 1 hour.
8. Preheat the Wood Pellet Smoker and Grill on smoke setting to 165 degrees F, using charcoal.
9. Arrange the salmon fillets onto the grill, skin side down and cook for about 3-5 hours or until desired doneness.
10. Remove the salmon fillets from grill and serve hot.

Nutritional Information per Serving:

- Calories 379
- Total Fat 10.5 g
- Saturated Fat 1.5 g

- Cholesterol 75 mg
- Sodium 14000 mg
- Total Carbs 26.8 g
- Fiber 0.1 g
- Sugar 25.3 g
- Protein 41.1 g

Sesame Seeds Flounder

Preparation Time: 15 minutes
Cooking Time: 2½ hours
Servings: 4

Ingredients:

- ½ cup sesame seeds, toasted
- ½ teaspoon kosher salt flakes
- 1 tablespoon canola oil
- 1 teaspoon sesame oil
- 4 (6-ounce) flounder fillets

Method:

1. Preheat the Wood Pellet Smoker and Grill on grill setting to 225 degrees F.
2. With a mortar and pestle, crush sesame seeds with kosher salt slightly.
3. In a small bowl, mix together both oils.
4. Coat fish fillets with oil mixture generously and then, rub with sesame seeds mixture.
5. Place fish fillets onto the lower rack of grill and cook for about 2-2½ hours.
6. Remove the fish fillets from grill and serve hot.

Nutritional Information per Serving:

- Calories 343
- Total Fat 16.2 g
- Saturated Fat 2.3 g
- Cholesterol 116 mg
- Sodium 476 mg
- Total Carbs 4.2 g
- Fiber 2.1 g
- Sugar 0.1 g
- Protein 44.3 g

Citrus Salmon

Preparation Time: 15 minutes
Cooking Time: 30 minutes
Servings: 6

Ingredients:

- 2 (1-pound) salmon fillets
- Salt and ground black pepper, as required
- 1 tablespoon seafood seasoning
- 2 lemons, sliced
- 2 limes, sliced

Method:

1. Preheat the Wood Pellet Smoker and Grill on grill setting to 225 degrees F.
2. Season the salmon fillets with salt, black pepper and seafood seasoning evenly.
3. Place the salmon fillets onto the grill and top each with lemon and lime slices evenly.
4. Cook for about 30 minutes.
5. Remove the salmon fillets from grill and serve hot.

Nutritional Information per Serving:

- Calories 327
- Total Fat 19.8 g
- Saturated Fat 3.6 g
- Cholesterol 81 mg
- Sodium 237 mg
- Total Carbs 1 g
- Fiber 0.3 g
- Sugar 0.2 g
- Protein 36.1 g

Parsley Prawn Skewers

Preparation Time: 15 minutes
Cooking Time: 8 minutes
Servings: 5

Ingredients:

- ¼ cup fresh parsley leaves, minced
- 1 tablespoon garlic, crushed
- 2½ tablespoons olive oil
- 2 tablespoons Thai chili sauce
- 1 tablespoon fresh lime juice
- 1½ pounds prawns, peeled and deveined

Method:

1. In a large bowl, add all ingredients except for prawns and mix well.
2. In a resealable plastic bag, add marinade and prawns.
3. Seal the bag and shake to coat well
4. Refrigerate for about 20-30 minutes.
5. Preheat the Wood Pellet Smoker and Grill on grill setting to 450 degrees F.
6. Remove the prawns from marinade and thread onto metal skewers.
7. Arrange the skewers onto the grill and cook for about 4 minutes per side.
8. Remove the skewers from grill and serve hot.

Nutritional Information per Serving:

- Calories 234
- Total Fat 9.3 g
- Saturated Fat 1.7 g
- Cholesterol 287 mg
- Sodium 562 mg
- Total Carbs 4.9 g
- Fiber 0.1 g
- Sugar 1.7 g
- Protein 31.2 g

Buttered Clams

Preparation Time: 15 minutes
Cooking Time: 8 minutes
Servings: 6

Ingredients:

- 24 littleneck clams
- ½ cup cold butter, chopped
- 2 tablespoons fresh parsley, minced
- 3 garlic cloves, minced
- 1 teaspoon fresh lemon juice

Method:

1. Preheat the Wood Pellet Smoker and Grill on grill setting to 450 degrees F.
2. Scrub the clams under cold running water.
3. In a large casserole dish, mix together remaining ingredients.
4. Place the casserole dish onto the grill.
5. Now, arrange the clams directly onto the grill and cook for about 5-8 minutes or until they are opened. (Discard any that fail to open).
6. With tongs, carefully transfer the opened clams into the casserole dish and remove from the grill.
7. Serve immediately.

Nutritional Information per Serving:

- Calories 306
- Total Fat 17.6 g
- Saturated Fat 9.9 g
- Cholesterol 118 mg
- Sodium 237 mg
- Total Carbs 6.4 g
- Fiber 0.1 g
- Sugar 0.1 g
- Protein 29.3 g

Buttered Shrimp

Preparation Time: 15 minutes
Cooking Time: 30 minutes
Servings: 6

Ingredients:

- 8 ounces salted butter, melted
- ¼ cup Worcestershire sauce
- ¼ cup fresh parsley, chopped
- 1 lemon, quartered
- 2 pounds jumbo shrimp, peeled and deveined
- 3 tablespoons BBQ rub

Method:

1. In a metal baking pan, add all ingredients except for shrimp and BBQ rub and mix well.
2. Season the shrimp with BBQ rub evenly.
3. Add shrimp in the pan with butter mixture and coat well.
4. Set aside for about 20-30 minutes.
5. Preheat the Wood Pellet Smoker and Grill on grill setting to 250 degrees F.
6. Place the pan onto the grill and cook for about 25-30 minutes.
7. Remove the pan from grill and serve hot.

Nutritional Information per Serving:

- Calories 462
- Total Fat 33.3 g
- Saturated Fat 20.2 g
- Cholesterol 400 mg
- Sodium 485 mg
- Total Carbs 4.7 g
- Fiber 0.2 g
- Sugar 2.1 g
- Protein 34.9 g

Chapter 8: Vegetarian Recipes

Spiced Mushrooms

Preparation Time: 15 minutes
Cooking Time 45 minutes
Servings: 4

Ingredients:

- 4 cups fresh whole baby Portobello mushrooms, cleaned
- 1 tablespoon canola oil
- 1 teaspoon granulated garlic
- 1 teaspoon onion powder
- Salt and ground black pepper, as required

Method:

1. Preheat the Wood Pellet Smoker and Grill on smoke setting to 180 degrees F, using charcoal.
2. In a bowl, add all ingredients and mix well.
3. Place the mushrooms onto the grill and cook for about 30 minutes.
4. Remove the mushrooms from grill.
5. Now, preheat the grill on grill setting to 400 degrees F.
6. Place the mushrooms onto the grill and cook for about 15 minutes.
7. Remove the mushrooms from grill and serve warm.

Nutritional Information per Serving:

- Calories 50
- Total Fat 3.7 g
- Saturated Fat 0.3 g
- Cholesterol 0 mg
- Sodium 43 mg
- Total Carbs 3.3 g
- Fiber 0.8 g
- Sugar 1.6 g
- Protein 2.4 g

Mac n' Cheese

Preparation Time: 15 minutes
Cooking Time: 1 hour 10 minutes
Servings: 10

Ingredients:

- 2 pounds elbow macaroni
- ¾ cup butter
- ½ cup flour
- 1 teaspoon dry mustard
- 1½ cups milk
- 2 pounds Velveeta cheese, cut into ½-inch cubes
- Salt and ground black pepper, as required
- 1½ cups cheddar cheese, shredded
- 2 cups plain dry breadcrumbs
- Paprika, as required

Method:

1. Preheat the Wood Pellet Smoker and Grill on grill setting to 350 degrees F.
2. In a large pan of lightly salted boiling water, cook the macaroni for about 7-8 minutes.
3. Drain the macaroni well and transfer into a large bowl.
4. Meanwhile, in a medium pan, melt ½ cup of butter over medium heat.
5. Slowly, add the flour and mustard, beating continuously until smooth.
6. Cook for about 2 minutes, beating continuously.
7. Slowly, add milk, beating continuously until smooth.
8. Reduce the heat to medium-low and slowly, stir in Velveeta cheese until melted.
9. Stir in salt and black pepper and remove from the heat.
10. Place the cheese sauce over cooked macaroni and gently, stir to combine.
11. Place the macaroni mixture into greased casserole dish evenly and sprinkle with cheddar cheese.
12. In a small frying pan, melt the remaining 4 tablespoons of butter.
13. Stir in breadcrumbs and remove from heat.
14. Place the breadcrumbs mixture over cheddar cheese evenly and sprinkle with paprika lightly.

15. Place the casserole dish onto the grill and cook for about 45-60 minutes, turning the pan once halfway through.
16. Remove from the grill and serve hot.

Nutritional Information per Serving:

- Calories 914
- Total Fat 42.3 g
- Saturated Fat 24.6 g
- Cholesterol 122 mg
- Sodium 1600 mg
- Total Carbs 99.9 g
- Fiber 4.1 g
- Sugar 12 g
- Protein 37.2 g

Parmesan Cauliflower

Preparation Time: 15 minutes
Cooking Time: 45 minutes
Servings: 5

Ingredients:

- 1 whole cauliflower head
- ¼ cup olive oil
- Salt and ground black pepper, as required
- ½ cup butter, melted
- ¼ cup Parmesan cheese, shredded
- ½ tablespoon fresh parsley, chopped
- 2 garlic cloves, minced

Method:

1. Preheat the Wood Pellet Smoker and Grill on grill setting to 450 degrees F.
2. Coat the cauliflower head with olive oil and season with salt and black pepper generously.
3. Place the cauliflower head in a cast iron skillet.
4. Place the pan onto the grill and cook for about 25 minutes or until golden brown.
5. Meanwhile, in a small bowl, add the butter, Parmesan, parsley and garlic and mix well.
6. Remove the pan from grill and coat the cauliflower with butter mixture evenly.
7. Place the pan onto the grill and cook for about 20 minutes.
8. Remove from the grill and place the pan set aside for about 5 minutes.
9. Cut the cauliflower head into desired-sized wedges and serve.

During the last 20 minutes of cooking, baste the cauliflower with the melted butter mixture.

Nutritional Information per Serving:

- Calories 281
- Total Fat 29.6 g
- Saturated Fat 13.8 g
- Cholesterol 52 mg
- Sodium 246 mg
- Total Carbs 3.4 g

- Fiber 1.4 g
- Sugar 1.3 g
- Protein 2.8 g

Mixed Veggies Combo

Preparation Time: 15 minutes
Cooking Time: 30 minutes
Servings: 8

Ingredients:

- 4 cups butternut squash, peeled, seeded and chopped
- 2 cups fresh shiitake mushrooms, sliced
- 1 small yellow cauliflower head, stem removed and cut into 2-inch florets
- 1 small purple cauliflower head, stem removed and cut into 2-inch florets
- 3 tablespoons olive oil
- Salt and ground black pepper, as required
- ½ cup Parmesan cheese, shredded
- ¼ cup fresh parsley, chopped finely

Method:

1. Preheat the Wood Pellet Smoker and Grill on grill setting to 500 degrees F.
2. In a large bowl, add vegetables, oil, salt and black pepper and toss to coat well.
3. Divide the vegetables onto 2 baking sheets and spread in an even layer.
4. Place the baking sheets onto the grill and cook for about 20-30 minutes, stirring once after 15 minutes.
5. Remove the vegetables from grill and transfer into a large bowl.
6. Immediately, add the Parmesan and parsley and toss to coat well.
7. Serve immediately.

Nutritional Information per Serving:

- Calories 118
- Total Fat 6.8 g
- Saturated Fat 1.6 g
- Cholesterol 4 mg
- Sodium 129 mg
- Total Carbs 12.6 g
- Fiber 3.3 g
- Sugar 3.5 g
- Protein 4.5 g

Cheesy Potato Fries

Preparation Time: 15 minutes
Cooking Time: 21 minutes
Servings: 5

Ingredients:

- 4 Yukon gold potatoes
- 2 tablespoons olive oil
- 1 tablespoon garlic, minced
- 2 teaspoons onion powder
- ½ teaspoon red pepper flakes, crushed
- Salt and ground black pepper, as required
- 2 cups cheddar cheese, shredded
- 2 tablespoons fresh chives, chopped

Method:

1. Preheat the Wood Pellet Smoker and Grill on grill setting to 500 degrees F.
2. Cut each potato into 8 equal-sized wedges.
3. In a large bowl, add potato wedges and remaining ingredients and toss to coat well.
4. Arrange the potato wedges onto the grill and cook for about 8 minutes per side.
5. Remove the potato wedges from grill and place into a greased cast iron skillet.
6. Sprinkle the potato wedges with cheddar cheese evenly and place the skillet onto the grill.
7. Cook for about 5 minutes more.
8. Remove from the grill and serve hot.

Nutritional Information per Serving:

- Calories 340
- Total Fat 20.8 g
- Saturated Fat 10.4 g
- Cholesterol 47 mg
- Sodium 326 mg
- Total Carbs 26.4 g
- Fiber 2 g
- Sugar 1.6 g
- Protein 14.3 g

Baked Beans

Preparation Time: 15 minutes
Cooking Time: 3 hours 5 minutes
Servings: 10

Ingredients:

- 1 tablespoon butter
- ½ of red bell pepper, seeded and chopped
- ½ of medium onion, chopped
- 2 jalapeño peppers, chopped
- 2 (28-ounce) cans baked beans, rinsed and drained
- 8 ounces pineapple chunks, drained
- 1 cup BBQ sauce
- 1 cup brown sugar
- 1 tablespoon ground mustard

Method:

1. Preheat the Wood Pellet Smoker and Grill on grill setting to 220-250 degrees F.
2. In a non-stick skillet, melt butter over medium heat and sauté the bell peppers, onion and jalapeño peppers for about 4-5 minutes.
3. Remove from heat and transfer the pepper mixture into a bowl.
4. Add remaining ingredients and stir to combine.
5. Transfer the mixture into a Dutch oven.
6. Place the Dutch oven onto the grill and cook for about 2½-3 hours.
7. Remove from the grill and serve hot.

Nutritional Information per Serving:

- Calories 364
- Total Fat 9.8 g
- Saturated Fat 3.8g
- Cholesterol 11 mg
- Sodium 1036 mg
- Total Carbs 61.4 g
- Fiber 9.7 g
- Sugar 23.5 g
- Protein 9.4 g

Vegetarian Pot Pie

Preparation Time: 15 minutes
Cooking Time: 1 hour 25 minutes
Servings: 10

Ingredients:

- 2 tablespoons cornstarch
- 2 tablespoons water
- 3 cups chicken broth
- 1 cup milk
- 3 tablespoons butter
- 1 tablespoon fresh rosemary, chopped
- 1 tablespoon fresh thyme, chopped
- Salt and ground black pepper, as required
- 2¾ cups frozen chopped broccoli, thawed
- 3 cups frozen peas, thawed
- 3 cups chopped frozen carrots, thawed
- 1 frozen puff pastry sheet

Method:

1. Preheat the Wood Pellet Smoker and Grill on grill setting to 375 degrees F.
2. In a small bowl, dissolve cornstarch in water. Set aside.
3. In a pan, add broth, milk, butter and herbs over medium heat and bring to a boil.
4. Add the cornstarch mixture and stir to combine well.
5. Stir in salt and black pepper and remove from the heat.
6. In a large bowl, add the vegetables and milk sauce and mix well.
7. Transfer mixture into a cast iron skillet.
8. With the puff pastry, cover the mixture and cut excess from edges.
9. Place the skillet onto the grill and cook for about 80 minutes.
10. Remove the pan from grill and set aside for about 15 minutes before serving.
11. Cut the pie into desired-sized portions and serve.

Nutritional Information per Serving:

- Calories 257
- Total Fat 14 g
- Saturated Fat 5 g

- Cholesterol 11 mg
- Sodium 408 mg
- Total Carbs 26.1 g
- Fiber 4.7 g
- Sugar 5.8 g
- Protein 7.6 g

Tofu Skewers

Preparation Time: 15 minutes
Cooking Time: 35 minutes
Servings: 3

Ingredients:

- 1 (14-ounce) block extra-firm tofu, pressed, drained and cut into 1-inch thick cubes
- 1 scallion, sliced thinly
- 1 garlic clove, minced
- ½ cup hoisin sauce
- 3 tablespoons rice wine vinegar
- 2 tablespoons soy sauce
- 1 tablespoon fresh lime juice
- 1 teaspoon sesame oil
- 1 teaspoon sesame seeds, toasted

Method:

1. In a bowl, place all ingredients except for tofu and sesame seeds and and mix until well combined.
2. Add the tofu cubes and coat with the sauce mixture generously.
3. Refrigerate to marinate overnight, gently tossing occasionally.
8. Preheat the Wood Pellet Smoker and Grill on smoke setting to 180 degrees F, using charcoal.
4. Remove the tofu cubes from bowl, reserving the marinade.
5. Thread the tofu onto pre-soaked skewers.
6. Place the skewers onto the grill and cook for about 10-15 minutes.
7. Remove the skewers from the grill.
8. Now, preheat the grill on grill setting to 400 degrees F.
9. Place the skewers onto the grill and cook for about 20 minutes, rotating the skewers every 5 minutes and brushing with the reserved marinade.
10. Remove the skewers from grill and place onto a platter.
11. Garnish with sesame seeds and serve.

Nutritional Information per Serving:

- Calories 253
- Total Fat 11.2 g

- Saturated Fat 1.2 g
- Cholesterol 1 mg
- Sodium 1302 mg
- Total Carbs 23.3 g
- Fiber 2.1 g
- Sugar 12.6 g
- Protein 15.5 g

Potato Casserole

Preparation Time: 20 minutes
Cooking Time: 3 hours
Servings: 10

Ingredients:

- 5 tablespoons olive oil, divided
- 6 cups onions, sliced thinly
- 1 tablespoon fresh thyme, chopped and divided
- Salt and ground black pepper, as required
- 1 tablespoon unsalted butter
- 1¼ pounds Yukon gold potatoes, peeled and 1/8-inch thick sliced
- ½ cup heavy cream
- 2¼ pounds tomatoes, cut into ¼-inch thick slices

Method:

1. In a large cast iron pan, heat 3 tablespoons of oil and over high heat and cook onions, 1 teaspoon of thyme, salt and black pepper for about 5 minutes, stirring occasionally.
2. Reduce the heat to medium.
3. Add the butter and cook for about 15 minutes.
4. Reduce the heat to low and cook for about 10 minutes.
5. Preheat the Wood Pellet Smoker and Grill on grill setting to 350 degrees F.
6. Meanwhile, in a bowl, add potatoes slices, cream, 1 teaspoon of thyme, salt and black pepper and toss to coat.
7. In another bowl, add tomato slices, salt and black pepper and toss to coat.
8. Transfer half of the caramelized onions into a small bowl.
9. In the bottom of the cast iron pan, spread the remaining onion slices evenly and top with 1 layer of potatoes and tomatoes.
10. Drizzle with 2 tablespoons of cream from potato mixture and 1 tablespoon of olive oil.
11. Sprinkle with a little salt, black pepper and ½ teaspoon of thyme.
12. Spread remaining caramelized onions on top, followed by potatoes and tomatoes.
13. Drizzle with remaining cream from the potatoes and remaining tablespoon olive oil.
14. Sprinkle with a little salt, black pepper and remaining ½ teaspoon of thyme.

15. With a piece of foil, cover the cast iron pan tightly.
16. Place the pan onto the grill and cook for about 2 hours.
17. Remove from grill and uncover the cast iron pan.
18. Now, set the grill to 450 degrees F.
19. Place the cast iron pan, uncovered onto the grill and cook for about 25-30 minutes.
20. Remove from grill and serve hot.

Nutritional Information per Serving:

- Calories 154
- Total Fat 10.7 g
- Saturated Fat 3.2 g
- Cholesterol 11 mg
- Sodium 36 mg
- Total Carbs 14.6 g
- Fiber 3.1 g
- Sugar 5.8 g
- Protein 2.3 g

Cheesy Corn

Preparation Time: 15 minutes
Cooking Time: 2 hours
Servings: 12

Ingredients:

- 2 tablespoons butter
- ½ of green bell pepper, seeded and chopped
- ½ of red bell pepper, seeded and chopped
- ½ of onion, chopped
- 52-ounce frozen corn
- 3-4 cup cheddar cheese, shredded
- 8 ounces cream cheese, softened
- Salt and ground black pepper, as required

Method:

1. Preheat the Wood Pellet Smoker and Grill on grill setting to 275-350 degrees F.
2. In a skillet, melt the butter over medium heat and sauté the bell peppers and onion for about 4-5 minutes.
3. Remove from the heat and stir in remaining ingredients.
4. Transfer the mixture into an aluminum pan evenly.
5. Place the pan onto the grill and cook for about 1-2 hours, stirring after every 30 minutes.
6. Remove the pan from grill and serve hot.

Nutritional Information per Serving:

- Calories 774
- Total Fat 25.7 g
- Saturated Fat 12.6 g
- Cholesterol 56 mg
- Sodium 357mg
- Total Carbs 127.7 g
- Fiber 18.4 g
- Sugar 22.6 g
- Protein 30.3 g

Chapter 9: Extra Recipes

Apple Pie

Preparation Time: 15 minutes
Cooking Time: 55 minutes
Servings: 8

Ingredients:

For Filling:

- 1 (9-inch) frozen double crust
- ¾ cup sugar
- 1 tablespoon all-purpose flour
- 1 teaspoon ground cinnamon
- Pinch of salt
- 3½ cups, cooking apples, peeled, cored and chopped
- 16 ounces applesauce
- 1 tablespoon fresh lemon juice
- 2 tablespoons cold butter, chopped

For Topping:

- 3 tablespoons all-purpose flour
- 1 tablespoon sugar
- Pinch of salt
- 1 tablespoon butter

Method:

1. Preheat the Wood Pellet Smoker and Grill on grill setting to 400 degrees F.
2. Place half of dough in the bottom of a 9-inch pie plate.
3. For topping: in a bowl, mix together sugar, flour, cinnamon and salt.
4. Add apples, applesauce and lemon juice and stir to combine.
5. Place apple mixture into pie pan and top with butter in the shape of dots.
6. Cut remaining crust into strips and place over pie in a lattice pattern.
7. For topping: in a bowl, mix together flour, sugar and salt.
8. With a fork, cut in butter until a crumbly mixture is formed.
9. Sprinkle topping mixture over top of crust evenly.

10. Place the pie plate onto the grill and cook for about 10 minutes.
11. Now, set the grill to 350 degrees F and cook for about 45 minutes.
12. Remove from the grill and place the pie onto a wire rack to cool in the pan for about 10 minutes.
13. Cut into desired-sized slices and serve warm.

Nutritional Information per Serving:

- Calories 233
- Total Fat 5.4 g
- Saturated Fat 3 g
- Cholesterol 11 mg
- Sodium 270 mg
- Total Carbs 44.3 g
- Fiber 1.5 g
- Sugar 28.2 g
- Protein 3.9 g

Rhubarb Crunch

Preparation Time: 15 minutes
Cooking Time: 1 hour
Servings: 8

Ingredients:

- 1 cup oatmeal
- 1 cup flour
- 1 cup brown sugar
- ½ cup butter, melted
- ¼ teaspoon salt
- 4 cups raw rhubarb, chopped finely
- 1 cup white sugar
- 2 tablespoons cornstarch
- 1 cup cold water
- 1 teaspoon vanilla extract

Method:

1. Preheat the Wood Pellet Smoker and Grill on grill setting to 350 degrees F.
2. In a bowl, add oatmeal, flour, brown sugar, butter and salt and mix until well combined.
3. In a pan, add white sugar, cornstarch, cold water and vanilla extract and cook until sugar is dissolves, stirring continuously.
4. Place half of the four mixture into a 9x12-inch pan and top with chopped rhubarb evenly.
5. Place sugar mixture over rhubarb evenly and top with remaining flour mixture.
6. Place the pan onto the grill and cook for about 1 hour.
7. Remove from the grill and place the crunch onto a wire rack to cool in the pan for about 10 minutes.
8. Cut into desired-sized slices and serve warm.

Nutritional Information per Serving:

- Calories 382
- Total Fat 12.5 g
- Saturated Fat 7.5 g
- Cholesterol 31 mg

- Sodium 164 mg
- Total Carbs 66.3 g
- Fiber 2.6 g
- Sugar 43.5 g
- Protein 3.7 g

Irish Soda Bread

Preparation Time: 15 minutes
Cooking Time: 1½ hours
Servings: 10

Ingredients:

- 4 cups flour
- 1 cup raisins
- ½ cup sugar
- 1 tablespoon caraway seeds
- 2 teaspoons baking powder
- 1 teaspoon baking soda
- ¾ teaspoon salt
- 1¼ cups buttermilk
- 1 cup sour cream
- 2 eggs

Method:

1. Preheat the Wood Pellet Smoker and Grill on grill setting to 350 degrees F.
2. Grease a 9-inch round cake pan.
3. Reserve 1 tablespoon of flour in a bowl.
4. In a large bowl, mix together remaining flour, raisins, sugar, caraway seeds, baking powder, baking soda and salt.
5. In another small bowl, add buttermilk, sour cream and eggs and beat until well combined.
6. Add egg mixture into flour mixture and mix until just moistened.
7. With your hands, knead the dough until sticky.
8. Place the dough into the prepared pan evenly and cut a 4x¾-inch deep slit in the top.
9. Dust the top with reserved flour.
10. Place the pan onto the grill and cook for about 1½ hours or until a toothpick inserted in the center comes out clean.
11. Remove from grill and place the pan onto a wire rack to cool for about 10 minutes.
12. Carefully, invert the bread onto the wire rack to cool completely before slicing.
13. Cut the bread into desired-sized slices and sere.

Nutritional Information per Serving:

- Calories 340
- Total Fat 6.6 g
- Saturated Fat 3.5 g
- Cholesterol 44 mg
- Sodium 361 mg
- Total Carbs 63 g
- Fiber 2.2 g
- Sugar 20.3 g
- Protein 8.6 g

Conclusion

The ketogenic barbecue diet is one of the most popular weight loss programs in the world due to its ability to melt away fat, boost energy levels, and sharpen your focus. If you've put off trying the keto barbecue diet for fear of missing out on your favorite foods, fear no more. This keto barbecue cookbook provides the means to empower everyone to develop a customizable approach plan, offering many options while dealing with the limitations of the standard ketogenic diet. And all that without sacrificing on Taste or Quality!

If you're looking for a Keto BBQ cookbook that includes delicious recipes with step-by-step instructions, then look no further! You don't have to be a professional cook nor diet expert to enjoy all those great meals. Just take this book, put it into action and Enjoy!

www.ingramcontent.com/pod-product-compliance
Lightning Source LLC
Chambersburg PA
CBHW081404070526
44583CB00020B/2665